DEVOS FOR BRAVE BOYS

DEVOS FOR BRAVE BOYS

JESSE FLOREA AND KAREN WHITING

Tyndale House Publishers
Carol Stream, Illinois

Visit Tyndale online at tyndale.com.

Visit Tyndale's website for kids at tyndale.com/kids.

Tyndale is a registered trademark of Tyndale House Ministries. The Tyndale Kids logo is a trademark of Tyndale House Ministries.

Devos for Brave Boys

For manufacturing information regarding this product, please call 1-855-277-9400.

For information about special discounts for bulk purchases, please contact Tyndale House Publishers at csresponse@tyndale.com, or call 1-855-277-9400.

ISBN 978-1-4964-5116-3

Printed in the United States of America

27 26 25 24 23 22 21
 7   6   5   4   3   2   1

NOT AFRAID

Read about trusting God during hard times in Psalm 31.

RESEARCHERS SAY PEOPLE LIKE FEELING SCARED—as long as there's no real danger. That's why riding roller coasters, skydiving, and adrenaline-filled sports are so popular (of course, some of those activities can actually be dangerous). But many times frightening images, especially from movies or the internet, can get stuck in our brains, causing us to have bad dreams or be afraid.

Instead of getting caught up in scary or evil stuff, God wants us to focus on him. He doesn't want us to be afraid. He came to cast out fear. Psalm 118:6 says, "The LORD is for me, so I will have no fear. What can mere people do to me?" Because God lives in us through the Holy Spirit, we have no reason to be afraid. Our eternity is secure with our heavenly Father. We may have moments of fear, but deep down we should know that with God on our side, we don't need to stay afraid.

Instead of being fearful, ask God to help you stand out in the world by living fearlessly. Be courageous. Be bold. Be excited about God. If you have friends who struggle with fear, tell them about the peace that comes from knowing the one and only Savior.

Pray: Tell God you're going to stand in his truth and not get sucked into the culture of fear.

Be strong and courageous, all you who put your hope in the LORD!
PSALM 31:24

SNAKE IN THE GRASS

Read about Adam and Eve's disobedience in Genesis 2:4–3:7.

SOME SNAKES JUST LOOK SCARY. When a king cobra rises up and displays its diamond-shaped hood, you naturally want to run. Other snakes *sound* mean. You *never* want to be close enough to hear a rattlesnake shake its tail. Then there are the colorful snakes. These striped serpents can be deadly, like the coral snake, or perfectly harmless, like the scarlet king snake. A good rule to follow if you see a red, black, and yellow striped snake is "Red next to yellow kills a fellow. Red next to black is a friend to Jack." But unless you're an expert, it's probably best not to pick up snakes no matter what color they are.

God created the beautiful Garden of Eden and told Adam he could eat from any tree except the tree of the knowledge of good and evil. Then a snake (you may know him better as Satan) tempted Eve into eating from the tree, saying, "Your eyes will be opened as soon as you eat [the fruit], and you will be like God, knowing both good and evil" (Genesis 3:5). Of course, it was a lie. Eve and Adam both disobeyed God, fell for the temptation, and ate the fruit. The consequences were huge. It messed up their relationship with God and brought sin into the world, and they were kicked out of the Garden.

You will also be tempted to disobey God and to think you know better than he does. Don't give in. God wants the best for you. Obey him, knowing that he has a way more amazing life planned for you than you could ever imagine for yourself.

Pray: Thank God for being your Creator and Savior. Tell him that you want to follow him.

> *"You won't die!" the serpent replied to the woman. "God knows that your eyes will be opened as soon as you eat it, and you will be like God, knowing both good and evil."*
> **GENESIS 3:4-5**

PUZZLE IT OUT: MAKING THE RIGHT CHOICES

Decide if each activity is a good or bad choice. Circle the letter under the column you choose.

	Good	Bad
Cleaning your room	P	N
Letting a friend copy your homework	U	S
Throwing stones at a neighbor's car	M	A
Reading the Bible	L	B
Helping your mother cook dinner	M	E
Lying	2	1
Cheating in a game	3	1
Going to church	9	5

Now fill in the blanks with the letters or numbers you circled to find verses about wise choices.

___ ___ ___ ___ ___   ___ ___ ___:9-11

What do these verses tell you about making good choices?

_____

_____

_____

_____

3

SEARCH AND FIND: SNAKES IN A GAME

Look for these dangerous snakes in the grass. Search up, down, across, diagonally, and backward.

T	B	L	A	C	K	M	A	M	B	A
A	I	T	R	A	S	K	B	V	G	D
I	V	G	W	R	I	U	P	N	W	D
P	T	I	E	J	K	V	A	C	O	O
A	D	D	E	R	A	L	I	T	C	R
N	E	K	A	N	S	L	A	R	O	C
O	X	A	C	M	P	N	U	S	B	P
C	T	Q	O	B	N	M	A	L	R	L
K	W	O	R	P	S	P	E	K	A	E
Z	B	L	A	N	K	V	I	P	E	R
R	A	T	T	L	E	S	N	A	K	E

Adder
Black Mamba
Cobra
Taipan
Viper
Asp
Boomslang
Coral Snake
Tiger Snake
Rattlesnake

HIDE-AND-SEEK GONE WRONG

Read about Adam and Eve hiding from God in Genesis 3:8-24.

HAVE YOU EVER PLAYED HIDE-AND-SEEK? What's the best hiding place you've ever found? Don't write it down—you may want to use that spot again.

A girl in Utah discovered the worst place to hide when she climbed into her family's washing machine during a game in January 2014. (She must *not* have read the warning label.) The eleven-year-old did a good job staying out of sight, but then she realized she was stuck. She screamed for help, and her family came running. They tried pouring water on her and smearing her with peanut butter to get her out. Nothing worked. So they called 911. Firefighters came to her rescue and had to dismantle the machine to set her free. At first, her legs didn't work because of severe cramping, but she eventually started walking fine and didn't have to go to the hospital.

Hide-and-seek can be fun as long as you don't hide in a dangerous place . . . or try to hide from God. That's what Adam and Eve learned in Genesis 3. After they sinned, the couple sewed fig leaves together as clothes and hid when the Lord walked through the Garden of Eden. God easily found them and called them out on their sin.

When you break one of God's laws, don't hide from him—run toward him! Boldly confess your sin to God and ask for forgiveness. Hiding will do you no good, especially if you sneak inside a washing machine.

Pray: Ask God to expose any hidden sin you have in your life. Pray for forgiveness, and promise not to hide from God.

> *If we confess our sins to him, he is faithful and just to forgive us our sins and to cleanse us from all wickedness. If we claim we have not sinned, we are calling God a liar and showing that his word has no place in our hearts.*
> 1 JOHN 1:9-10

COOL CRUISE

Read about Noah building a huge boat in Genesis 6:5-22.

AT THE TIME the cruise ship *Oasis of the Seas* motored into the ocean for the first time, it was the world's largest passenger ship. More than six thousand people could fit on this floating fun park—and that doesn't count the 2,394 crew members. The ship is more than three football fields long, 20 stories high, and over 200 feet wide.

While the sheer size of the *Oasis of the Seas* is impressive, what it holds is even better! There's a carousel, a zip line, two surfing wave pools, a mini-golf course, a basketball court, two rock-climbing walls, a kids' water park, and an ice-skating rink. More than three thousand construction workers took about two years to finish this ship at a cost of $1.5 billion.

The Bible talks about a great ship too. But instead of being built for fun, it was built for survival. In Genesis, God tells Noah that the world is so evil that he's going to send a flood to kill "every living thing that breathes" (Genesis 6:17). He gave Noah plans to build an ark. The Bible doesn't say exactly how long it took him to build it, but it was probably at least fifty years! Even though the ark was massive—450 feet long, 75 feet wide, and 45 feet high—and held two of every animal, it was less than half the size of today's cruise ships. Of course, it held only eight people, not eight thousand!

Noah built the ark just as God instructed, and God blessed Noah's obedience. The ark kept Noah, his family, and all the animals safe when water covered the earth for 150 days.

Pray: Ask God to help you obey his commands, even if they don't make sense to you.

God wiped out every living thing on the earth—people, livestock, small animals that scurry along the ground, and the birds of the sky. All were destroyed. The only people who survived were Noah and those with him in the boat.
GENESIS 7:23

QUIZ TIME:
GET TOGETHER

Animals like to hang out in groups. Sometimes those groups have funny names. Draw a line from the animal to its group name. Then check your answers to see how many you got right.

Animal	Name of Group
Cow	Mob
Goose	Pod
Whale	Gaggle
Crow	Herd
Kangaroo	Pack
Monkey	Troop
Wolf	Murder
Lion	Pride

PUZZLE IT OUT: KEY TO SUCCESS

Answer these math problems and fill in the correct word to complete Proverbs 13:13:

"People who despise advice are asking for trouble; _____ _____
                                                        11 - 9   1 + 2

_____ ____ _____ _____ _____."
     1 x 1   2 x 3   49 ÷ 7   15 - 11   45 ÷ 9

1. respect
2. those
3. who
4. will
5. succeed
6. a
7. command

8

HIGHER CALLING

Read about Abram leaving his home and bravely following God's instructions in Genesis 12:1-9.

WHAT HAVE YOU been called to?

a. A life that honors God
b. Treating others with kindness
c. Passing along the Good News about Jesus
d. Dinner
e. All of the above

The answer is e. Following your calling is sometimes difficult. (Unless it's being called to dinner. That's easy. All you need is a fork.) God doesn't call us to an easy life. But when we follow him, he promises to bless us.

That was certainly the case for Abram. At the beginning of Genesis 12, God tells him: "I will make you into a great nation. I will bless you and make you famous, and you will be a blessing to others" (verse 2). That's certainly a great calling. Who wouldn't want to be famous and bless others? But God says something *before* that awesome message. In verse 1, he tells Abram to leave his country and family and move to a different land.

Any move is difficult, but this one proved to be especially hard. Abram and Sarai experienced a bunch of bumps in the road. They didn't do a perfect job of following God's plan. But they always came back to the Lord and trusted him to fulfill his promise. And in case you were wondering, Abram *did* become a great nation, *is* still very famous, and *was* a blessing to others.

Pray: Ask God to help you find his calling. Then pray for the courage to follow it.

I will make you into a great nation. I will bless you and make you famous, and you will be a blessing to others.
GENESIS 12:2

FLOATING FIRE

Read about God's promise to Abram in Genesis 15:1-19.

WHAT WOULD YOU RATHER SEE: a beautiful rainbow in the sky or a flaming torch floating between two halves of a cut-open animal? One of those images is beautiful and inspiring. The other is just plain disgusting.

But in the first book of the Bible, God shows his faithfulness in keeping his promises by using both a rainbow and a floating torch. While these images may stir up very different mental pictures, the meaning is the same for both: God always comes through.

After God flooded the earth, he put a rainbow in the sky and promised Noah that he'd never flood everything again. In Genesis 9:14-15, God says, "When I send clouds over the earth, the rainbow will appear in the clouds, and I will remember my covenant with you and with all living creatures. Never again will the floodwaters destroy all life." What a beautiful picture!

The picture isn't quite as beautiful six chapters later when God promised Abram that he'd have as many descendants as there were stars in the sky. Even though Abram was old and didn't have any children, he believed God. Abram sacrificed several animals to the Lord, as was the custom of the time, and then at night he saw "a smoking firepot and a flaming torch pass between the halves of the carcasses" (Genesis 15:17). That floating fire confirmed in Abram's heart that God had truly made a covenant with him. To Abram, it was as beautiful as seeing a rainbow.

The Bible is filled with God's promises. Mark them in your Bible when you read it, and thank God that he can be trusted to keep every single one.

Pray: Praise God for never breaking his promises.

> [God said,] "No, I will not break my covenant; I will not take back a single word I said."
> **PSALM 89:34**

EXPERIMENT:
HOMEMADE RAINBOW

Since it's too dangerous to play with flaming torches, make this rainbow to remember that God always keeps his promises.

STUFF YOU NEED
- CD
- Flashlight

TRY IT
1. Go into a dark room.
2. Hold the CD in one hand and the flashlight in the other.
3. Shine the flashlight at the bottom of the CD. Move it around at different angles (and closer to and farther from the CD), and watch a rainbow appear.

LIFTOFF LIST

Abram heard directly from God about his calling. Check off all the ways God may call you:

_____ Talents and passions

_____ Encouragement from friends or family members

_____ Bible verses

_____ Answered prayer

_____ An unexpected opportunity

_____ A favorite subject in school

TOUGH TEST

Read about Abraham* preparing a sacrifice in Genesis 22:1-19.

YOU WALK INTO MATH CLASS and see two dreaded words written on the board: *Pop Quiz!* "Okay, class," your teacher says. "If you pass this quiz, you get an A for the semester. But if you don't do well, you'll receive an F on your report card."

You look at the paper. Only two questions. The first says, "An alley separates two tall buildings. Engineers decide to attach cables to the buildings for strength. The cables go from the base of one building to the roof of the other and crisscross in the middle. One of the cables is 240 feet. The other is 160 feet. If the cables crisscross 40 feet above the ground, how wide is the alley?"

The other question is just an equation:

$$\text{If } \underline{\hspace{4cm}} \text{ , then } q = \underline{\hspace{2cm}} \text{ .}$$

That's so unfair, you think. *There's no way I can pass this test.*

Abraham was probably thinking the same thing when God gave him a pop quiz to test his faith. But his test was way harder. In the beginning of Genesis 22, God tells Abraham to sacrifice his beloved son, Isaac. Abraham had seen God do amazing things and bless him immeasurably. Now God was asking him to do the unthinkable.

The Bible doesn't tell us if Abraham had to think twice about God's request. It just says Abraham got up, saddled his donkey, chopped some firewood, and headed toward Mount Moriah. Just as Abraham was about to strike Isaac down, God provided a different sacrifice. The Bible says Abraham's faith pleased God. God is still pleased when we show faith in him by rising up to a difficult test.

Pray: Ask God to strengthen your faith in him.

Some time later, God tested Abraham's faith. "Abraham!" God called. "Yes," he replied. "Here I am."
GENESIS 22:1

---

* God changed Abram's name to Abraham in Genesis 17:5.

WRESTLING AN ANGEL

Read about Jacob's all-night wrestling match in Genesis 32:22-32.

WOULD YOU EVER wrestle with an angel? Not if you were smart. It'd be sort of like grappling against all the strongest, biggest professional wrestlers in the world . . . at the same time. There's just no way you could win. But one man in the Old Testament wrestled an angel and won—sort of.

One night Jacob prayed for God's help. Later that night, a man came and wrestled with Jacob. They struggled all night. At daybreak the man could tell Jacob wasn't giving up. The man touched Jacob's hip, causing it to dislocate. Still, Jacob clung to the man and asked for a blessing, because Jacob knew the man was really an angel. The angel blessed him and changed his name to Israel. He said that Jacob had fought with God and with men and won (Genesis 32:28). *Hooray!* God blessed him. But the angel's touch changed Jacob, and he limped from that day on.

Israel means "God fights" or "He struggles with God." The name Israel reminded Jacob of his struggle for the rest of his life. Sometimes living the Christian life feels like a struggle. When we prayed to accept Christ, Jesus didn't promise an easy life. In fact, he said the opposite. The Lord said the world may hate us. We'll have to overcome obstacles. But God also promised that he'll be with us every step of the way and that he'll help us overcome (see John 16:33).

When you pray for God to answer a prayer, don't give up if you can't see an answer right away. It's okay to struggle and wrestle with God. He wants you to be persistent. Keep believing, and keep asking for his blessing.

Pray: Pray again for a prayer that hasn't been answered yet. Be persistent.

Jacob struggled with the Angel and prevailed.
HOSEA 12:4, HCSB

AWESOME ACTIVITY: PRAYER KEEPER

God is a prayer keeper. He always hears and answers your prayers. Sometimes he answers yes right away. Sometimes he says no. Sometimes he asks you to wait. As followers, we have to trust that God's timing is perfect.

Get a spiral notebook to keep track of your prayers. Write the date and what you pray. After a while, look back and write down how God answered your prayers. Share with others how he answered, and then watch your faith—and theirs—grow stronger.

PUZZLE IT OUT:
MISSING WORD

First Thessalonians 5:17 is one of the shortest and most powerful verses in the Bible. Look at the words below. One letter from each of the first words is missing from the second set of words. Write that letter in the matching space to discover the missing word from the verse.

1. pecan   cape
2. cream   cram
3. over   ore
4. floor   fool

"__ __ __ __ __ stop praying." — 1 Thessalonians 5:17
  1   2   3   2   4

SOARING WITH EAGLES

Read about God's protection in Psalm 91.

HAVE YOU EVER wanted to stay in bed and not get up for the day? Young eaglets feel that way. They'd rather stay in a soft nest than venture into the world. They might never try to fly if not for their wise mothers. A mother eagle stirs up the nest by pulling out everything soft. She tosses out feathers, animal skin, and anything else that is cozy. Soon the eaglets wiggle around looking for a soft place to rest, but the sticks and thorns in the nest hurt and make them uncomfortable. The mother eagle then spreads her wings wider than the nest, and one of the eaglets gingerly steps onto a wing. The mother flutters her wings, and the baby tightens its claws to cling to her feathers. The mother soars into the air, carrying the eaglet high above the earth. Then she lurches and the eaglet topples off her wing. The little eaglet flops, tumbles, and rolls. It beats its wings in the air. About halfway back to earth, the mother bird swoops down and collects the eaglet back onto her wing. She soars upward again and repeats the process until the little bird learns to fly.

Sometimes God is like a mother eagle. He urges us to trust him and move out of our comfort zones. Maybe he pushes us to try something new. And when we are afraid, he carries us. Even if it feels as if we are tumbling and falling, God will always catch us. He never stops caring for us as he teaches us to soar with him.

Pray: Ask God to give you the courage to follow him and the ability to trust him in any situation.

> [The Lord] was like an eagle that stirs up its nest. It hovers over its little ones. It spreads out its wings to catch them. It carries them up in the air on its feathers.
> **DEUTERONOMY 32:11,** NIRV

BROTHER TROUBLE

Read about Joseph's brothers selling him into slavery in Genesis 37:18-36.

WHAT'S THE DEAL with biblical brothers? If you're looking for good examples on how to live with your siblings, you may have difficulty finding them in the Bible. Cain and Abel were the first two brothers—and one of them ended up dead. *Yikes!* Then there's Joseph and his brothers. Genesis 37 tells us how Joseph's brothers wanted to kill him because he was their father's favorite. (Those dreams Joseph had about his brothers bowing to him didn't help matters either.) Just before they were about to do the deed, the oldest brother, Reuben, spoke up and said they should throw Joseph into a pit instead. After they threw him into the hole, a group of traders came by on their camels.

"Instead of hurting our brother, let's sell him to those traders," Joseph's brother Judah suggested. So that's what they did. Talk about brotherly *un*love.

If you have brothers or sisters, they probably bother you from time to time. Joseph's brothers focused on all the things they didn't like about him instead of his positive qualities. That caused them to make a very bad decision. Think about your siblings. What do you appreciate the most about them? Write down a few ideas:

1. _____

2. _____

3. _____

God wants us to live in harmony with our family members. We can do that by remembering that these are lifelong relationships. Your siblings will probably be there for you even longer than your parents. If you fight with your siblings, forgive. If you argue, agree to end things on a good note. Even when it's hard, commit to building strong relationships with your siblings.

Pray: Ask God to give you the patience and wisdom to live in peace with your siblings.

How wonderful and pleasant it is when brothers live together in harmony!
PSALM 133:1

QUIZ TIME:
OH, BROTHERS

Draw a line to connect the biblical brothers.

Cain	Aaron
Joseph	Andrew
Jacob	Abel
Moses	Esau
Peter	Reuben

AWESOME ACTIVITY: HELP YOUR FAMILY BE STRONGER

Help your family be stronger with these tips:

- Give your mom (or another family member) a hug every day.
- Spend time with your family.
- Listen and encourage family members to follow their dreams.
- Pray with and for your family.
- Communicate and let your family know your plans, feelings, and dreams.
- Thank family members for their actions and even for listening to you.
- Forgive family members who hurt you.
- Pitch in to help around the house.

RUNNING AWAY

Read about God's faithfulness to Joseph in prison in Genesis 40.

HAVE YOU EVER found yourself in a situation where your friends wanted you to do something you knew was wrong? How did you respond?

The Bible tells us that running away from trouble is often the right choice. That's what Joseph did in the Old Testament. He had been taken to Egypt and forced to work for Potiphar, the captain of the guard. One day Potiphar's wife wanted Joseph to do something wrong, but Joseph refused to sin against God. Joseph ended up in trouble with his boss, but it was not his fault. Potiphar's wife lied to make her husband angry, and Potiphar tossed Joseph into prison. Joseph didn't give a list of excuses—just accepted the punishment.

Years later, God allowed Joseph to be released from prison, and Joseph ended up in a great place with lots of money and power. God had better plans for Joseph than Joseph could have dreamed of, even though he went through years of difficulties and problems first.

Sometimes we have to find the courage to turn from trouble and run. We may lose friends or feel lonely for a while, but we can trust God to be with us and bring new friends and better situations into our lives.

Pray: Ask God to give you the wisdom and courage to run from evil.

Run from all these evil things. Pursue righteousness and a godly life, along with faith, love, perseverance, and gentleness.
1 TIMOTHY 6:11

NOTHING UP MY SLEEVE—PRESTO!

Read about God calling Moses to save his people from Egypt in Exodus 3:1–4:17.

THOUSANDS OF YEARS AGO, the Israelites lived as slaves in Egypt. They cried out to God, and God called Moses to go free his people. Just one problem: Moses didn't want to do it. Even though God had uniquely prepared him by having him grow up in Pharaoh's palace, Moses was scared to return. He didn't think the Egyptians would listen to him. After all, he'd fled Egypt after killing a man. Plus, he didn't speak well. Instead of relying on the God of the universe, Moses came up with excuses.

God didn't listen to Moses' excuses. He simply told Moses to toss his staff on the ground. *Hiss!* It turned into a snake. Then he told Moses to pick up the snake by the tail. Presto! It was a shepherd's staff again. Next, God told Moses to put his hand into his cloak. When he pulled it out, he was holding a beautiful bouquet of flowers. Wrong! His hand was actually white with disease. Moses put his hand back into his cloak, and this time it came out perfectly healed.

But God knew Moses was the right man for the job. God was compassionate to Moses and promised to help him before Pharaoh. Moses responded by trusting God and going to Egypt.

God wasn't concerned about Moses' ability; he wanted Moses' *availability* to follow him. And that's the same thing God wants from you.

Pray: Tell God you want to do his will for your life—no excuses.

> *God also said to Moses, "Say this to the people of Israel: Yahweh, the God of your ancestors—the God of Abraham, the God of Isaac, and the God of Jacob—has sent me to you."*
> **EXODUS 3:15**

LIFTOFF LIST

Just like he did for Moses, God has special plans for your life. There are some things that he wants all of his followers to do. Other times God has specific tasks just for you.

Read this list of a few things that God wants all Christians to do. Then write in a couple ideas of how God might be specifically calling *you*.

Tell your family and friends about God.
Obey your parents.
Be generous with your money.
Pray and read your Bible.
Keep your promises.
Be kind to others.

_____.

_____.

_____.

_____.

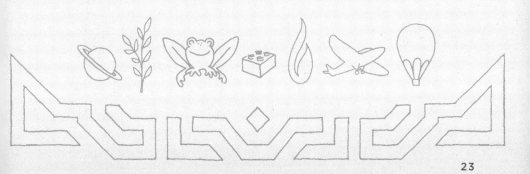

PUZZLE IT OUT:
UNLOCK THE TRUTH

God has given you many talents and abilities. To get the most out of them and make the biggest difference in the world, you have to use your gifts for God's glory. Unlock your future by figuring out the message on this combination lock. Just "spin" it to the left (L) or right (R), starting at the letter *O* at the top, and write the correct letters in the spaces below.

L-4, R-1, L-3, R-5, L-6, R-2,   L-6, R-2, L-8

___ ___ ___ ___ ___ ___   ___ ___ ___.

BULLIES WITH CHARIOTS

Read the song the Israelites sang to God after he saved them from the Egyptians in Exodus 15:1-21.

PHARAOH WAS A BIG BULLY. As the leader of Egypt, he forced God's people to work for him as slaves for many years. When God sent Moses to ask Pharaoh to let his people go, Pharaoh said, "No!" Then he made the people work even harder.

God changed Pharaoh's mind after sending lots of problems on the Egyptians. Pharaoh was no match for God's power—not to mention all the flies; gnats; and dead camels, donkeys, and cows God used to show his might to Pharaoh. At last, Moses led the people out of captivity and toward the Promised Land.

Oops! Instead of really letting God's people go, Pharaoh decided to bully them one more time. The Israelites had to walk, but Pharaoh had chariots and weapons. He led his army against the Israelites.

Pharaoh thought his chariots and army were mightier than Israel's God. *Wrong!* God performed a few miracles at just the right time. God parted the Red Sea to let his people walk across and escape. Pharaoh's army galloped after them. *Splash! Crash!* God closed the sea. Water flowed and covered the entire army. God destroyed Pharaoh's army and kept his people safe.

The Israelites celebrated their freedom from the Egyptians. They sang, danced, and ate. But mostly, they praised God for saving them.

Pray: Praise God for his mighty power.

When Pharaoh's horses, chariots, and charioteers rushed into the sea, the LORD brought the water crashing down on them. But the people of Israel had walked through the middle of the sea on dry ground!
EXODUS 15:19

GRUMBLING MUMBLES

Read about the Israelites grumbling against God right after he rescued them from Egypt in Exodus 16.

"IT'S MY TURN!"

"Why do I have to take out the garbage?"

"Can't you buy me that new video game? Everyone else has it."

It's easy to complain and argue. But it doesn't make life very peaceful. When you constantly grumble, you can cause yourself—or the people around you—to become angry. The word *anger* comes from a Greek term that means "to lose control." God doesn't want you to be out of control. He desires for us to show self-control as much as we can.

In the Old Testament, the Israelites grumbled a lot. This usually showed that they didn't believe God would take care of them—but he always did. They grumbled when they were thirsty or hungry, and God provided food and water. God had plans to care for his people when he freed them from slavery in Egypt. He just wanted them to trust him. Often they didn't.

We can't always see God's plans for us, but we can trust him to have our best interests in mind, because he does. The Bible tells us to "do everything without complaining and arguing" (Philippians 2:14). When you grumble in discontent, it shows that you don't trust God. God may not give you everything at the exact time that you want it, but just like your parents, he will supply what you need. So enjoy what you already own. Praise God for your blessings, and strive to be happy and content. And if anybody hears a grumble coming from you, it should just be from your hungry stomach.

Pray: Ask God to give you the strength to be content with what you have and not complain or argue.

Do everything without complaining and arguing.
PHILIPPIANS 2:14

PUZZLE IT OUT: THANKSGIVING ACROSTIC

Fill in the blanks with things you can be thankful for. Thank God for them, and think of other blessings for which you can be thankful.

1.	T ___ ___ ___	Items to play with
2.	H ___ ___ ___	Where you live
3.	___ A ___ ___ ___ ___	The people who live with you
4.	___ ___ ___ N ___ ___ ___	Your homeland
5.	___ ___ ___ K ___	You read these
6.	S ___ ___ ___ ___ ___	Where students learn
7.	G ___ ___	He made you
8.	___ ___ I ___ ___ ___ ___	Pals
9.	___ ___ V ___	Parents give you this from their hearts
10.	___ ___ I ___ ___	You believe, so you have this
11.	___ ___ ___ ___ ___ N	Where believers live forever
12.	G ___ ___ ___ ___	You play these

Answers: 1. Toys; 2. Home; 3. Family; 4. Country; 5. Books; 6. School; 7. God; 8. Friends; 9. Love; 10. Faith; 11. Heaven; 12. Games

WACKY LAUGHS

Try these jokes with friends and family.

Q. What do you call a complaining lawn?
A. Crab grass.

Q. What was the taxi driver's problem?
A. He was always driving away his customers.

Q. What lives in a hive and always complains?
A. Grumble bees.

Q. Which animal complains the most?
A. The whine-oceros.

POWERFUL DRONE FORCE

Read about God choosing Joshua as the leader of the Israelites in Joshua 1:1-9.

BUZZ! ZAP! Modern-day drone airplanes whirl through the sky and strike enemy forces with unexpected power.

When God's people entered the Promised Land, there was nothing like today's high-tech drone strike force. Instead God chose another type of drone—male bees and hornets—to win battles for his people. God used these tiny dive-bombers to attack the enemy. Swarms of hornets charged from the sky and stung the Israelites' enemies (Joshua 24:12, NIV).

While God provided firepower from the air, Joshua led his people from the ground. Joshua wasn't your typical leader; he was born a slave and then helped Moses for forty years. Also, the Israelites had no time to build war machines. God gave them unusual weapons—like a swarm of hornets, or horns whose blasts could break down walls. Not normal battle strategies, but God's way showed the people their victories were not due to their own strength but to his.

God's first words to Joshua were "Be strong and courageous" (Deuteronomy 31:23). He told Joshua to obey his commands. God promised to be with Joshua wherever he went. That great pep talk let Joshua know he could count on God's help.

Joshua led the army and won many battles as he relied on God's strength.

Pray: Ask God for strong faith in him.

This is my command—be strong and courageous! Do not be afraid or discouraged. For the Lord your God is with you wherever you go.
JOSHUA 1:9

HOPE ON A ROPE

Read about Joshua sending spies into Jericho in Joshua 2.

HAVE YOU EVER TRIED to climb a rope in gym class or scale a climbing wall like Spider-Man? It's not easy. You have to possess superstrong hand and forearm muscles to grip tightly and climb safely.

Before God's people went into the Promised Land, Joshua sent two spies to scope things out near Jericho. The spies snuck into the city, but Jericho's king found out and wanted them captured. Soldiers searched for the spies and learned they'd visited a woman named Rahab. Rahab told the soldiers that the spies had left the city, but they were actually hidden on her roof. Once the king's men were gone, Rahab tied a rope securely to her window—which was in the city wall.

"I know the Lord has given you this land," she said to the spies. "We are afraid of you. So when you capture the city, swear you'll save me and my family."

The spies agreed and quickly climbed down the rope to safety. They returned to Joshua and told him, "All the people in the land are terrified of us" (Joshua 2:24). They also explained to Joshua how Rahab had bravely saved them from being captured and the promise they made to her. Joshua honored that promise after the walls around Jericho fell.

Pray: Thank God that he can win battles for us before they even start.

Since Rahab's house was built into the town wall, she let them down by a rope through the window.
JOSHUA 2:15

EXPERIMENT: STRONG PAPER

Paper is easy to cut and rip, yet it can surprise you with its strength.

STUFF YOU NEED
- Paper
- Sharp knife
- Potato

TRY IT
Fold the paper in half around the sharp side of the knife. Slice a potato by holding the handle of the knife but not touching the paper. *Surprise!* The knife cuts the potato but not the paper, because the potato is softer than the paper fiber.

AWESOME ACTIVITY: CLIMB ON

If you want to become an excellent climber, try these easy exercises to strengthen the muscles you use for climbing.

- Grip strength helps you hold things. Find an old tennis ball or racquetball. Squeeze it 15 times with each hand. Repeat three times.
- Flexibility is key for climbers. See if you can stand and touch your toes. Hold for seven seconds.
- Strong shoulders help you hold yourself up. Grab two full gallon-size milk jugs. Hold them at your sides. Shrug your shoulders straight up, and hold for a few seconds. Lower them straight down. Do 10 repetitions.
- Build your core strength with sit-ups, crunches, or planks. A strong core helps with every activity.

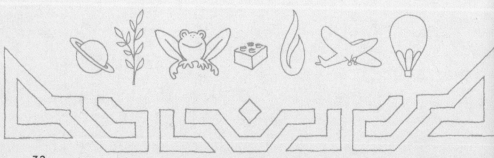

UNLIKELY HERO

Read about the signs God showed Gideon in Judges 6.

WHY ARE THEY ALWAYS PICKING ON US? Gideon thought.

He shook in his sandals as he hid in a hole from the powerful Midianites. The Midianites had stolen wheat from the Israelites for seven years. Gideon hoped to keep some grain for himself. As he hid, he tossed pieces of wheat up in the air to separate the grain from the part you can't eat, called chaff. But wheat needs a breeze to blow away the chaff. Breezes don't blow in holes in the ground. Things weren't going well for Gideon.

Suddenly, an angel appeared.

"Mighty hero, the Lord is with you!" the angel said to Gideon.

Gideon looked around. Nobody else was in the hole, so he figured the angel was talking to him.

"Why is God letting our enemies hurt us?" Gideon asked. "Where is he?"

Then the Lord spoke. "I'm sending you."

"I'm so little, from the weakest family in the whole country," Gideon argued.

"I'll be with you," the Lord said.

Gideon wanted proof to be sure he had heard God. He placed meat and bread on a rock as a gift to the Lord. God sent fire to consume the food.

Gideon asked for more signs. He laid a wool fleece (a sheepskin) on the ground. God let dew wet the fleece but not the ground. The next night God kept the fleece dry and wet the ground. Finally, Gideon fought back his fears. He would trust God to help him stand up to the bullies. God gave Gideon the confidence to be a leader. And God wants you to be a leader today.

Pray: Ask God to help you be brave and trust him, even if you don't think you are the bravest, strongest, or biggest guy around.

> *"But Lord," Gideon replied, "how can I rescue Israel? My clan is the weakest in the whole tribe of Manasseh, and I am the least in my entire family!"*
> **JUDGES 6:15**

NOISY BATTLE

Read about the Israelite victory over the Midianites in Judges 7.

GIDEON SNUCK INTO THE MIDIANITE CAMP to spy. He and his soldiers were terribly outnumbered—300 versus more than 100,000. But Gideon and his men had the Lord on their side. Gideon crept close to a tent and overheard a soldier tell his friend about a dream. In the dream the man saw a loaf of barley bread knock over a Midianite tent. *Hooray!* God had sent the dream as a sign of victory for the Israelites.

Gideon returned to his men and shouted, "Get up! God has given us the victory!" They prepared for a midnight raid by going to grab their weapons. But instead of spears and shields, Gideon gave the men horns and torches inside clay jars. Gideon split his men into three groups. The men followed Gideon and surrounded the Midianite camp. Gideon blew his trumpet and smashed his jar. He grabbed the torch and held it high.

All Gideon's men smashed their jars and shouted, "A sword for the Lord and for Gideon!" The noise woke the enemy; it sounded like a huge army surrounded them. The Midianites shook in their sleeping bags. When they peeked out of their tents, they saw bright flashes of light from the torches. Now they were sure a huge army was coming after them.

The Midianites grabbed their swords and stabbed at anything near them. *Oops!* They even stabbed one another. Terrified by all the noise and chaos, they ran away. God's chosen men had won the battle, thanks to the Lord!

Pray: Thank God that he lets you participate in his victories.

It was just after midnight, after the changing of the guard, when Gideon and the 100 men with him reached the edge of the Midianite camp. Suddenly, they blew the rams' horns and broke their clay jars.
JUDGES 7:19

WACKY LAUGHS

Knock, knock.
Who's there?
Dew?
Dew who?
Dew drop in and visit!

Q. What did the dew say when it formed on the grass?
A. Nothing, it just dew-dled.

Q. Why did bread falling on a tent worry the Midianites?
A. They thought they would be sandwiched.

Q. What did the Midianites say after they lost the battle?
A. "What a jarring experience!"

Q. When did modern sound systems begin?
A. In Bible days. Gideon used surround sound to win a battle.

EXPERIMENT:
CREATE SOUND EFFECTS

Try making sound effects with items around the house. Here are some ideas:

- Snap carrots to make a bone-cracking sound.
- Create the sound of a fire crackling by wrinkling cellophane and snapping twigs.
- Drop a sack of potatoes for the sound of somebody tripping and hitting the floor.
- Flap heavy work gloves to create the sound of birds flapping their wings.
- Fill a box with rocks to drop for crashing sounds.
- Blow through a straw in a glass of water to make the sound of boiling water.

STRONG HAIR

Read about God using Samson in spite of his failures in Judges 16:4-30.

NO HAIRCUT FOR THAT BOY! An angel of the Lord told Samson's mother that she would have a special son. He would be very strong, and God would use him to be a special helper for the Israelites. But he must never get his hair cut, shave, or drink alcohol. The hair part sounds pretty weird, but Samson made a bold fashion statement wherever he went.

His actions were also bold. God used Samson to fight the Philistines. Ropes couldn't hold him. Neither could gates. Once the people in the town of Gaza planned to kill him, but Samson lifted the city gates—poles and all—and carried them to the top of a hill.

Samson was strong, but he had a weakness for women. He made bad choices when it came to women, including getting involved with one named Delilah.

The Philistines paid Delilah to find out the source of Samson's strength so they would have a chance at beating him. Once Delilah discovered Samson's hair was the root of his strength, she lulled him to sleep and had his head shaved. Then the Philistines poked out Samson's eyes and chained him to the pillars of their stronghold, a temple.

Samson was surrounded by more than three thousand people mocking him. He prayed for God to give him super strength just one more time. He realized his strength came from God—not his hair. Samson pushed apart the pillars of the temple and toppled the building. He wiped out more enemies than ever before. He died doing it, but he taught the enemy a lesson: God gives people strength when they need it.

Pray: Ask God to give you the strength and wisdom to trust him.

> Samson shared his secret with [Delilah]. "My hair has never been cut," he confessed, "for I was dedicated to God as a Nazirite from birth. If my head were shaved, my strength would leave me, and I would become as weak as anyone else."
> **JUDGES 16:17**

A SLING AND A PRAYER

Read about David bravely facing Goliath in 1 Samuel 17.

THINK OF THE BIGGEST GUY you've ever seen. Maybe he's a football player or professional wrestler. Now think of the meanest kid you know. Put those two thoughts together and what do you get?

Well, whatever you get, it probably wouldn't compare to nine-foot-tall Goliath. He stood meaner, bigger, and tougher than any other bully. What Goliath had in height, he lacked in intelligence. He only had one move—the old dare-ya trick. He would just yell, "*I dare* the soldiers of Israel to send a man down to fight me." And when you're as big, mean, and scary as Goliath, no one wants to fight you.

But when David looked at Goliath, he didn't see an unbeatable warrior. He saw a bully who mocked God. So David went to King Saul and asked to fight. At first Saul refused, but David convinced him. Saul gave David his own armor—"a bronze helmet and a coat of mail." David put it on and strapped on a sword. He tried walking, but the armor was too bulky. He knew armor couldn't protect him; only God could do that.

God enjoys showing his strength in our weakness. David, the young shepherd, wasn't intimidated by Goliath. He refused to wear heavy armor and didn't shrink away when Goliath shouted curses. Instead, he said he was coming in the name of the Lord and that God was the one Goliath would really have to fight. He picked up five stones as his ammunition, but he only needed one. *Swish!* The stone zipped through the air, hit the giant between the eyes, and killed him in one blow. Once David chopped off Goliath's head, the Israelite soldiers gained courage and chased after the army of Philistines.

Pray: Thank God that he wants to show his strength in your weakness.

[David said,] "The Lord who rescued me from the claws of the lion and the bear will rescue me from this Philistine!"
1 SAMUEL 17:37

EXPERIMENT: SLINGSHOT SURPRISE

Make your own miniature slingshot to play with.

STUFF YOU NEED

- Bobby pin (your mom might have one)
- Pliers
- Scissors
- Rubber band
- Tiny pieces of paper
- Targets (such as plastic cups)

TRY IT

1. Use the pliers to bend the bobby pin into a Y shape, forming the frame of the slingshot.
2. Cut the rubber band once so it's a line instead of a circle. Tie each end to one of the arms of the slingshot.
3. Ball up tiny pieces of paper, gather some targets (plastic cups work well), and pretend you're shooting rocks at Goliath.

WACKY LAUGHS

Q. Why was David able to kill Goliath with a sling?

A. Because he was only a stone's throw away.

Q. A shark chased three sea creatures: a flounder, an angelfish, and an eel. They came upon some rocks and decided to throw them at the shark. The flounder tossed a rock and missed. The angelfish threw a rock and missed. The eel threw a rock and hit the shark. *Smack!* The shark swam away. So what does this prove?

A. Let he who has no fin cast the first stone.

LET IT SNOW

Read David's bold prayer of confession in Psalm 51.

WHEN YOU THINK ABOUT APRIL, you probably picture blooming flowers and refreshing rains. But April has also seen its share of epic snowstorms.

Between April 19 and 21, 1893, over 30 inches of snow fell on St. Cloud, Minnesota. Twenty-four inches of snow fell in a single day. The wet, heavy snow closed down trains and made roads nearly impassable. Of course, people didn't drive cars until the 1900s, so horses could still sort of get around.

More recently, nearly three feet of snow fell from April 5 to 7, 2008, in South Dakota, Minnesota, and Wisconsin. Gusty winds made drifts more than six feet high and closed down schools and businesses for days.

It doesn't snow too often in the Holy Land, and usually only the mountains get any accumulation. But in Psalm 51, David writes about the snow. David was a man after God's own heart, but he also made plenty of mistakes. In this psalm, David asks for God's mercy. He says that the times he's disobeyed God's commands make him feel terrible and keep him up at night. He tells the Lord that he's a sinner and that he wants his joy back. And he writes these amazing words: "Wash me, and I will be whiter than snow" (Psalm 51:7).

Don't be afraid to boldly confess your sins to God and receive his mercy. He promises to forgive you and make you as pure as newly fallen snow.

Pray: Confess your sins to God.

Purify me from my sins, and I will be clean; wash me, and I will be whiter than snow.
PSALM 51:7

FAITHFUL HEROES

Read about several people who boldly trusted God in Hebrews 11.

WHAT DO YOU NEED TO DO to be a hero for God? List a few ideas:

1. _____

2. _____

3. _____

You probably didn't list lying, murder, or deceiving others, but that's what some men in the Bible did before they became heroes. Isaac lied when he called his wife his sister. David had another woman's husband killed to cover up his sin. Jacob deceived his father and brother to get a better inheritance. But they all repented and started following God more closely.

God called these men—and many others throughout history—to follow him. Newspapers and Craigslist weren't around, but God's advertisement may have looked like this:

Wanted: Men of faith willing to be teased, beaten, possibly sawed in half; may need to sleep in caves or holes in the ground, be imprisoned, and wear goatskins.

That sounds pretty tough . . . and gross (especially being sawed in half). But that was the fate of many of God's faithful followers. Hebrews 11 lists the members of God's Hall of Faith—men and women who lived their faith and said yes when God called them. They suffered through many of the situations listed in the advertisement.

This chapter of Hebrews also tells us that mighty things happened when these heroes believed: they shut mouths of lions, conquered kingdoms, escaped death, became mighty, and obtained promises. Being a hero means having faith in God and saying yes to him. That one word can make an ordinary young man extraordinary.

Pray: Ask God for the courage to follow him and say yes when he calls.

Faith shows the reality of what we hope for; it is the evidence of things we cannot see.
HEBREWS 11:1

EXPERIMENT: KEEP IT CLEAN

The Lord purifies you from your sins and washes you whiter than snow. He also takes your sins as far away from you as the east is from the west (Psalm 103:12). Try this experiment as a way to see how God cleans up your life.

STUFF YOU NEED

- Bowl of water
- Pepper
- Dish soap

TRY IT

1. Fill a bowl half full with water.
2. Sprinkle pepper all over the surface of the water. The more the better. The pepper represents sin in your life.
3. Put a drop of dish soap on your finger. The soap represents God.
4. Dip your soapy finger into the bowl. What happens to the surface of the water? When God comes into your life, that's how clean you become.

PUZZLE IT OUT: THE BIG IDEA

Fill in each blank with the missing letter to complete the words. Then unscramble those letters to find a word that describes the people listed in God's Hall of Faith in Hebrews 11. (Hint: The word is on page 42.)

s c o __ d e d
__ e l l o
__ n s t r u c t i o n s
__ n g e l
__ i n a l l y
__ h r e e
__ o l l o w i n g
__ n d e r

— — — — — — — — —

ENDLESS BUFFET

Read about Elijah and the widow of Zarephath in 1 Kings 17:8-16.

ALL YOU CAN EAT! Sounds great. You can fill your stomach with lots of choices on a long buffet.

Not everyone gets all the food they need, though. One out of nine people in the world are starving. They don't have enough food to keep their bodies alive. Even where you live, statistics show people are hungry. In a small town in Florida, a lady known as Miss Irene collects food for needy people. She hears about families who need help, then she fills baskets of food and knocks on their doors.

One time a woman answered and cried, "I didn't know what I would give my son tonight. I only had one cup of rice in the house. My husband just got a job, but he won't get paid for a week."

Miss Irene hugged the woman and gently told her, "We have a food pantry at the church, and there's always plenty. You just call if you need anything."

Hunger is not a new problem. In 1 Kings 17, the prophet Elijah met a widow gathering sticks. He asked her for water and a little bread.

"I don't have a single piece of bread in the house," she said. "And I have only a handful of flour left in the jar and a little cooking oil in the bottom of the jug. I was just gathering a few sticks to cook this last meal, and then my son and I will die" (verse 12).

How sad. But Elijah told the woman not to worry. He said her jars of oil and flour would not run out. *Hooray!* The containers didn't become empty until the famine ended. She and her son enjoyed an endless bread buffet.

God can supply our needs and also use other people to help. How has God provided for you? In what ways can you use what you have to help others?

Pray: Ask God to help you care about those in need like he does.

The Lord, the God of Israel, says: There will always be flour and olive oil left in your containers until the time when the Lord sends rain and the crops grow again!
1 KINGS 17:14

ROCKS ON FIRE!

Read about fire raining down on Elijah's sacrifice in 1 Kings 18:16-40.

IF YOU WANT TO START A WOOD FIRE, you probably don't want to dump a ton of water on the wood. Water makes it hard to light a fire. But that's exactly what God's prophet Elijah did, and he did it to prove a point about God's power.

Elijah came face-to-face with some strange dudes back in the day. These men believed an idol named Baal was a god. *That's bad.* They worshiped Baal and did not believe in the one true God. They cut themselves and burned their children as sacrifices to Baal. That's *really* bad! God loves us and never wants us to harm a child or ourselves.

Elijah proposed a test between God and Baal. On one side stood Elijah—God's lone prophet. On the other side stood 450 prophets of Baal. Elijah told them to stack up wood and an animal sacrifice. He'd do the same. Then each side would call to their god to send down fire. The god who did this would prove himself to be the one true God. All the people thought that was a good idea. The prophets of Baal prayed for a fire to burn their wood. Nothing happened. They cried out all day and cut themselves until their blood gushed out. But not one spark flew.

In the evening, Elijah made an altar of twelve stones to represent the tribes of Israel. He stacked his wood and laid a bull on top. Then he poured water over the wood three times. Elijah said one loud prayer, asking God to start a blazing fire. *Whoosh! Sizzle!* Fire came from heaven. God's fire burned up the wood, the stones, and even the water around the altar. Those rocks were literally on fire for God!

God wants you to have faith like Elijah and believe in his power to do the miraculous. Elijah did not fear the worshipers of Baal or have any doubts that God would ignite his sacrifice. He stepped out in faith in order to display God's glory to the people on the mountain, and God honored him for it. Elijah got to witness God's incredible power flashing down from heaven. Pray for the same faith in God! It will rock your world.

Pray: Ask God to set your heart on fire for him.

Immediately the fire of the LORD flashed down from heaven and burned up the young bull, the wood, the stones, and the dust. It even licked up all the water in the trench!
1 KINGS 18:38

AWESOME ACTIVITY:
MIRACLE TRACKER

Sometimes it can feel as if we don't have much. Just a small jar of oil. But God can multiply our little and turn it into a lot. Get a piece of paper and a pencil. Write down any time you can remember when God turned your little efforts into big rewards. When you're done, ask your parents and grandparents if they have any stories of God "multiplying oil."

PUZZLE IT OUT:
REBUS PICTURE PUZZLE

Solve the picture clues to find out more about Jesus.

GGG + US   🪵-L   👁️🍖-H   🍞

_____ _____, "____ _____ the _____

L+ 🔪 - kn

of _____."

48

KEEP IT SIMPLE

Read about Naaman being healed of a skin disease in 2 Kings 5:1-19.

WHAT HAPPENS TO A BLACK ROCK that's thrown into the Red Sea?
   It gets wet.

What happens to an angry, sick general who's dunked in the Jordan River seven times?
   He gets healed.

It's true. You can read the whole story in 2 Kings 5. Naaman was a mighty Aramean army commander. He had guided his troops to great victories over the Israelites. His wife even had a young Israelite girl for a slave. As powerful as Naaman was, though, his body felt weak because he suffered from leprosy. Leprosy is a disease that causes muscle weakness, yucky sores, and the loss of feeling in your arms and legs.

One day the slave girl told Naaman's wife about the prophet Elisha in Samaria. She knew Elisha could heal her master. Naaman talked to the Aramean king and got his permission to go to Israel to talk with Elisha. But instead of coming out to speak with Naaman, Elisha sent a messenger to say, "Go dunk seven times in the Jordan River. Then you will be healed."

The news should have excited Naaman, but it didn't. It made him mad. He had expected Elisha to come out, wave his hand, and heal him. Dipping in the dirty Jordan River did not sound like the recipe for healing. But before Naaman could rush back to Aram, his officers said, "If the prophet had told you to do something very difficult, wouldn't you have done it? So you should certainly obey him when he says simply, 'Go and wash and be cured!'" (2 Kings 5:13). Naaman couldn't argue against that reasoning. He went. He washed. He was cured. And he worshiped God (verse 15).

Sometimes we're willing to do something doubly tough for God, but we won't do the simple things he asks us to do (such as reading his Word, praying, and treating others with kindness). Naaman learned that simple obedience can produce miracles.

Pray: Tell God you're going to do the little things for him.

Naaman said, "Now I know that there is no God in all the world except in Israel."
2 KINGS 5:15

INVISIBLE CHARIOTS

Read about God's powerful army in 2 Kings 6:8-23.

YOU CAN'T FIGHT GOD. That's what the king of Aram discovered. Whenever he wanted to attack Israel, he made secret plans to mobilize his army. But there are no secrets from God. God knew the king's plans and told them to his prophet Elisha. Then Elisha informed the king of Israel, and Aram's schemes were foiled.

Finally, the king of Aram got upset. He decided to capture Elisha so he couldn't ruin Aram's strategies anymore. The Arameans had a huge army with many horses and chariots. They surrounded the city of Dothan, where Elisha was. Elisha's servant was worried. But the man of God could see things that others couldn't. He asked God to open his servant's eyes. Suddenly, the man saw that the hillside was covered with horses and chariots of fire. It was God's army.

The Aramean army decided to attack. They couldn't see God's warriors. *Zap!* Now they couldn't see anything at all. God had struck the enemy blind.

Elisha led the blind army into Samaria, Israel's capital city, where God restored their sight. "Let's kill them," the king of Israel said. But Elisha told the king to feed the enemy and send them home. The king followed his instructions, and the gangs of Arameans stopped bullying Israel.

God always wins. You may not be able to see God or his angels like Elisha could, but God sees you. When you pray, God can show you his answer and give you the help you need.

Pray: Thank God for protecting and providing for you.

Elisha prayed, "O Lord, open his eyes and let him see!" The Lord opened the young man's eyes, and when he looked up, he saw that the hillside around Elisha was filled with horses and chariots of fire.
2 KINGS 6:17

WEIRD FACTS: CHARIOTS

- The original Olympics included chariot races.
- Roman chariots with two horses were called *bigas*. A *triga* was a chariot with three horses.
- Four-horse chariots were called *quadrigas*. The strongest two horses pulled from the center. The other two horses were tied to the center horses with ropes and rode beside the center ones.
- Teams of horses move faster than one horse. Jesus sent his disciples out in teams too. How do you think it helps to do God's work as part of a team? If one person feels discouraged, the other can cheer him up. Have you ever worked for God on a team?

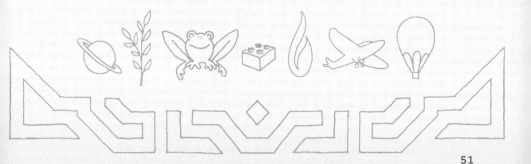

AWESOME ACTIVITY: JAZZ UP YOUR CHARIOT

Add some style to your bicycle with these ideas.

- Wrap tape around the handlebars or other parts of the bicycle.
- Stick decals on your helmet, and use paint or a permanent marker to add a design or your initials.
- Cut thin plastic straws (or coffee stirrers) into short pieces. Slice them open to make spoke covers to slip on your bicycle's wheels.

LOST AND FOUND

Read about Josiah leading the Israelites back to God in 2 Kings 22:1–23:3.

A SHEPHERD BOY IN ISRAEL was searching for a lost goat along crumbling cliffs near the Dead Sea. Suddenly, he spied a cave. Maybe you've had fun rock climbing with harnesses and strong ropes, but it's much scarier without places to grip and when rocks disintegrate as you try to grab them. The shepherd boy climbed to the mouth of the cave and tossed a rock inside. *Crash!* He heard something break. He left to tend his flocks and returned later with a friend. That's when they made an amazing discovery.

The boys entered the cave and found old jars they hoped contained great treasures. *Oomph!* They opened a tall clay jar and discovered old scrolls wrapped in linen. When Bible experts learned about the discovery, they rushed to the Qumran caves. These ancient papers, now called the Dead Sea Scrolls, turned out to be the oldest fragments of the Scriptures ever discovered.

When God's Word is found, it's a time to celebrate. In the Old Testament, King Josiah took over the throne after his father, evil King Amon, was killed. The people had forgotten God's Word and even lost the Scriptures, the law of Moses. As Josiah's workers restored the Temple, they found the law of Moses. Josiah read it and tore his clothes to show that he felt bad that he and his people had not followed God's Word. Josiah made changes and led his people in following God again.

Just like Josiah, you should listen to God's Word and allow it to change your heart. It took courage for Josiah to turn against the idolatry of his father and lead the Israelites back to God, but he did it anyway. He took God's Word seriously and was willing to do whatever it took to obey it.

How seriously do you take what you read in the Bible? When is the last time something in God's Word led you to change your actions? If it's been a while, ask God to make your heart soft toward him and his commands.

Pray: Ask God to help you obey his Word.

Never before had there been a king like Josiah, who turned to the LORD with all his heart and soul and strength, obeying all the laws of Moses. And there has never been a king like him since.
2 KINGS 23:25

QUIET HERO

Read about Mordecai asking Queen Esther to help save the Jews in Esther 4:1-17.

NO ONE EVEN LOOKED at the man as he sat by the gate. The man listened. He paced back and forth. He wrote letters. No sword, no shouting, no horseback riding. Doesn't sound like a hero, but God used this man, whose name was Mordecai, to help save thousands of people.

The king's advisor, Haman, hated Mordecai because Mordecai followed God and refused to bow down to Haman whenever he passed by. In fact, it made Haman so angry that he plotted to kill Mordecai and all of his people, the Jews. When Mordecai heard about Haman's plan, he sent a message to Queen Esther, his cousin, asking for her help.

Esther felt afraid, but Mordecai showed his great faith in God by saying that it was possible that she had become queen so she could save her people. His faith inspired Esther to action, and together they saved the Jewish people.

No matter if you consider yourself loud or quiet, funny or thoughtful, introverted or extroverted, God wants to use you. In the Bible, we see that God chooses all sorts of different people to accomplish his purposes and bring glory to him. How can you embrace the way God has created you and use your personality and gifts to faithfully serve him?

Pray: Thank God for creating you with unique gifts and purpose.

> [Mordecai said,] "If you keep quiet at a time like this, deliverance and relief for the Jews will arise from some other place, but you and your relatives will die. Who knows if perhaps you were made queen for just such a time as this?"
> **ESTHER 4:14**

PUZZLE IT OUT:
RIGHT DIRECTIONS

Cross out every *b*, *f*, *j*, *q*, *u*, *v*, *x*, and *z*. Then write the remaining letters in order below to discover how to trust God with your future.

b i j n a q l u l z t f h u y b w z a f y s
a j c k f j n o x f w b l e q f d g u f b e
h j f i b m a q u n b d v f z j h u e b b
z z s f b h a x q l l b f d q i x r e b c t
t b f h x z y p f b q a t z h f s b b f q z

"___ ____ ___ ____ _____

___,' ___ __ _____ _____ ___

_____."

AWESOME ACTIVITY:
VERSE CONCENTRATION

Use a game to help you remember Scripture verses.

STUFF YOU NEED

- Index cards
- Pen

TRY IT

1. Write each verse you want to memorize on two index cards (or print out verses and glue them on the cards). Make a stack of the pairs of verses.
2. Shuffle all the cards, turn them facedown, and lay them out.
3. Get a friend or a parent and play a game of Memory. Take turns flipping over cards and reading the verses to find a match.
4. Make it more challenging by writing half a verse on one card and the other half on another card. In this game, you must match up the two halves.

TRUSTING GOD NO MATTER WHAT

Read about Job praising God during very tough times in Job 1:1–2:10.

EVERYTHING THAT HAPPENS TO US on earth is real and significant. But sometimes we can forget that there's an even more important spiritual dimension to our lives. The book of Job reminds us of that fact. The Bible says Job feared God and stayed away from evil. And God blessed him for his actions. Job had 10 children, 7,000 sheep, 3,000 camels, and tons of servants, and he was one of the richest men in the land.

Job didn't keep his money to himself. He helped others. He gave to the poor and assisted orphans in need (Job 29:11-12). People respected Job because of the way he treated those around him.

While everybody else was impressed with Job, Satan wasn't. Satan said that the only reason Job served God was because God always protected and blessed him. So God allowed Satan to test Job. Job lost his animals, his servants, his health, and even his children. Satan thought Job would curse God if he lost everything. But Job didn't. He said, "Should we accept only good things from the hand of God and never anything bad?" (Job 2:10). Job continued to serve God and others. Later in his life, God blessed Job more than he had before. God gave him 14,000 sheep, 6,000 camels, and 10 more children.

You can learn a lot from Job's life. He praised God in the tough times. He understood life wasn't about riches; it was about serving God. And he used his blessings to bless others.

Pray: Ask God for the strength to trust him in good times and bad.

> *There once was a man named Job who lived in the land of Uz. He was blameless—a man of complete integrity. He feared God and stayed away from evil.*
> **JOB 1:1**

THE MASTER'S HANDS

Read about Jeremiah going to the potter's house in Jeremiah 18:1-11.

HAVE YOU EVER WATCHED a potter work at a pottery wheel? A master potter can turn a simple lump of clay into a beautiful creation. With just a slight squeeze of his hands, he can make a beautiful vase, useful bowl, or galloping pony. (Okay, he can't make a real pony.) A potter's skill shows in everything he makes.

In the book of Jeremiah, the Lord tells his prophet to go down to the potter's shop. At the shop, Jeremiah watches as the potter makes a jar. But the jar doesn't turn out the way the potter wants, so he smashes the clay back into a lump and starts again. Then the Lord says to Jeremiah, "Can I not do to you as this potter has done to his clay? As the clay is in the potter's hand, so are you in my hand" (Jeremiah 18:6).

When God works in your life, he forms you into something beautiful to be used in his Kingdom. It may take some pounding, squeezing, and spinning, but God is making you into something amazing. Does the clay tell the potter what to do? No. Does the clay complain that it wants to be a pony and not a pot? No.

As clay in the Master Potter's hands, we need to trust God with our lives.

Pray: Praise God that he's the Master Potter. Tell him that you trust him to make you what you should be.

> The Lord gave me this message: "O Israel, can I not do to you as this potter has done to his clay? As the clay is in the potter's hand, so are you in my hand."
> **JEREMIAH 18:5-6**

PUZZLE IT OUT

Answer the questions and read the shaded boxes to discover the missing word from this famous quote from Job.

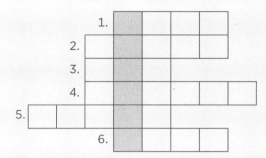

1. A group of wolves is called a _____.
2. The color of dirt.
3. You hit a baseball with a _____.
4. Opposite of big.
5. If you have a question, you _____ your hand.
6. You dye these at Easter.

"The LORD gave me what I had, and the LORD has taken it away. _____ the name of the LORD!" — Job 1:21

EXPERIMENT:
SLIMY SENSATION

Make your own claylike slime.

STUFF YOU NEED

- White glue
- Water
- Two bowls
- Borax laundry booster
- Food coloring
- Large spoon
- Plastic resealable bag

TRY IT

1. Mix four ounces of glue with a half cup of water. Stir in a couple drops of food coloring.
2. In another bowl, dissolve one teaspoon of borax in one cup of water.
3. Stir the glue mixture into the borax mixture. Keep stirring until your slime forms.
4. Remove the slime from the bowl and start playing. Store slime in a Ziploc bag.

NOT IN THE DARK

Read what it means to be a child of the light in 1 Thessalonians 5:5-11.

ARE YOU AFRAID OF THE DARK? Researchers say one in four kids is afraid of something. One of the most common fears is being left alone in the dark.

You probably know there are a lot of Bible verses about fear. God doesn't want you to be afraid. He wants you to trust him and overcome your fears. Isaiah 41:10 says, "Don't be afraid, for I am with you. Don't be discouraged, for I am your God. I will strengthen you and help you." Next time you're afraid, think about that verse, and be encouraged. God can give you the strength to beat your fears.

God also equips you to defeat the dark. In the book of 1 Thessalonians, the apostle Paul tells Christ's followers that they don't belong to the dark. They're children of the light. Isn't that cool? You're a child of the light! As a child of the light, you shouldn't have anything to do with darkness. And God provides armor to protect against the dark, including the helmet of salvation (Ephesians 6:17).

When you believe in Jesus as your Savior, he clothes you in armor. This armor protects you from darkness. It's armor built from faith and love, and it should make you confident to live for Christ. Sure, doubts, fears, and other attacks may come your way. But when they do, be confident of your salvation in Christ, and know that his light shines in you.

Pray: Thank God for his protective armor and ask him to give you the courage to not be afraid.

God is light, and there is no darkness in him at all.
1 JOHN 1:5

TWISTED TALE

Read about God calling Ezekiel to be a prophet using a fiery tornado in Ezekiel 1:4-14 and 2:1-7.

SEEING A TORNADO CAN BE SCARY. People say twisters scream across the ground like a freight train. But what if that freight train was on fire? *Yikes!* Fire tornadoes are much rarer than other tornadoes. Also called fire whirls, these natural phenomena form when intense hot air rises inside a wildfire. A fire twister can lift smoke, ash, and debris high in the air and spread the fire fast. As the air twirls and spins, it can grow and become larger and more dangerous. Fortunately, just like other tornadoes, fire tornadoes usually last only a couple of minutes.

In the Bible, the prophet Ezekiel described a strange, fiery windstorm (see today's verse). The windstorm Ezekiel saw sounds like a fire whirl. People rarely see them, although forest rangers may catch a glimpse of one more frequently. Ezekiel said that the center of the fire looked like glowing metal. If you've ever watched a blacksmith on a video or at a historic site put iron in a fire, you know the metal glows with intense heat. That's like what Ezekiel saw. This was the beginning of a vision God gave Ezekiel to reveal his glory and power.

God spoke to Ezekiel in this fiery vision. He called Ezekiel to be a prophet and to bravely report his words to the people. God may never speak to you in a vision, but he communicates with you in many other ways. You can hear God in his Word, through advice you get from a parent or grandparent, and in your heart from the Holy Spirit. Plus, you can see God's power in nature. It may not be in an awesome fire tornado, but God's power is evident even in a simple rainstorm.

Pray: Ask God to help you listen to his voice.

> *[Ezekiel said,] I looked up and saw a windstorm coming from the north. I saw a huge cloud. The fire of lightning was flashing out of it. Bright light surrounded it. The center of the fire looked like glowing metal.*
> **EZEKIEL 1:4**, NIRV

AWESOME ACTIVITY: GREAT GUIDE

Get a bandanna or other blindfold. Then find a friend, sibling, or parent and have them cover your eyes so you can't see. Have that person guide you from one room to another with just their voice. (Example: "Go forward three steps and stop. Now turn right and walk forward two steps.") See if you can make it without getting hurt. Then put your hand on your guide's shoulder, and without any talking, go where you are led. Take turns guiding each other, and then discuss these questions:

- What was easier to follow—instructions by voice or by touch?
- What were the challenges of each method?
- Was it hard to trust the person guiding you?
- How does God guide us?

PUZZLE IT OUT:
IT ALL ADDS UP

Solve these math problems, and then write in the correct word to discover what Moses told God's people when they were afraid.

"_____ _____ _____. _____ _____ _____ ___
   5 x 2   8 ÷ 4   2 x 3   15-6   21 ÷ 3   13-12   4 + 4

_____ _____ _____ _____ ____ _____." — Exodus 14:13
 16 ÷ 4   5 + 6   6 x 2   16-13   3 + 2   16-3

1 = still	4 = watch	7 = stand	10 = Don't
2 = be	5 = you	8 = and	11 = the
3 = rescue	6 = afraid	9 = Just	12 = LORD
			13 = today

Answer: "Don't be afraid. Just stand still and watch the LORD rescue you today."

RATTLING BONES

Read about the unusual vision God showed Ezekiel in Ezekiel 37:1-14.

YOU'VE LOST SOME BONES. Seriously! But don't worry. They aren't lying around somewhere. It's how God designed you. You were born with 300 bones. But as you've grown, some of your bones—especially in your skull—have fused together and become stronger. Right now you probably have 206 bones. That means you've lost 94 bones! That's a lot of bones. But it's nowhere near the number of bones the prophet Ezekiel saw in a strange vision.

Ezekiel saw a valley full of bones. God told him to speak to the bones, so he did: "Dry bones, listen to the word of the LORD!" (Ezekiel 37:4). Suddenly, the bones rattled and moved. *Yikes! Clank! Clink! Rattle!* The bones came together and formed complete skeletons. God told Ezekiel to speak over the bones again. Muscles grew onto the bones, and then skin grew. Then God told Ezekiel to say, "Come, O breath, from the four winds! Breathe into these dead bodies so they may live again" (verse 9). The bones came to life and formed a great army.

That story may give you the creeps, but God used it to bring hope to his people. Enemies had captured the Israelites. God's people had given up hope and said to one another, "We have become old, dry bones" (verse 11).

God can breathe his spirit of life into us when we feel depressed or think we have failed and nothing will get better. If you feel down with lazy bones, ask God to breathe life into your spirit.

Pray: Ask God to fill your spirit with hope and joy.

> *"I will put my Spirit in you, and you will live again and return home to your own land. Then you will know that I, the LORD, have spoken, and I have done what I said."*
> **EZEKIEL 37:14**

FIRE PROTECTION

Read about three friends who were willing to die for their faith in Daniel 3.

WHEN FIREFIGHTERS RUSH INTO BURNING BUILDINGS, they wear special suits to help them stay safe. These suits can protect them in temperatures of nearly 600 degrees. That's pretty amazing. But the shiny, heavy suits aren't flameproof, and they don't provide much protection against other dangers, such as smoke. That's why firefighters also carry compressed air into fires to help them breathe. Firefighting is a dangerous job, so thank these brave men and women whenever you see them.

When Shadrach, Meshach, and Abednego were thrown into the fiery furnace, they were not wearing fireproof suits. The Bible tells us they were tied up and tossed into the fire wearing pants, turbans, robes, and other clothing. Sounds like they'd immediately burst into flames. But that's not what happened. Their ropes burned away, and they walked around unharmed. When they were let out of the furnace, the Bible says that they didn't even smell of smoke! So what saved them?

In a word: God.

Before Nebuchadnezzar put Shadrach, Meshach, and Abednego in the fire, they said that the God they served could save them. Then they said these amazing words: "Even if he doesn't, we want to make it clear to you, Your Majesty, that we will never serve your gods" (Daniel 3:18). These brave young men were willing to die for their faith. They knew God could do anything. And God saved them. Now that's the ultimate fire protection!

Pray: Ask God to give you the courage to stand up for your beliefs—no matter the consequences.

Then Nebuchadnezzar said, "Praise to the God of Shadrach, Meshach, and Abednego! He sent his angel to rescue his servants who trusted in him. They defied the king's command and were willing to die rather than serve or worship any god except their own God."
DANIEL 3:28

AWESOME ACTIVITY: CANDY-ADE

Ezekiel shared that God would replace people's hard hearts with new ones that would not be like hearts of stone. Soften hard candy for a sweet drink.

STUFF YOU NEED

- 3 pieces of hard candy
- Plastic resealable bag
- Hammer
- Glass of water
- Baking soda and lemon juice (optional)

TRY IT

1. Place candies in a resealable bag.
2. Hammer candies to crush them into a powder.
3. Mix candies in a glass of water. This makes a sweet drink.
4. Stir in ½ teaspoon baking soda and 1 tablespoon lemon juice to make the drink fizz.

WEIRD FACTS:
THAT'S HOT!

- Candle flames burn at 1,800 degrees Fahrenheit.
- Fires need heat, fuel, and oxygen to burn.
- You should check the batteries in smoke alarms twice a year.
- Red fire is approximately 1,500 degrees Fahrenheit. Orange-colored flames are around 2,000 degrees. White flames can be 2,600 degrees or more!
- Always have an escape plan from your home in case of a fire. Talk to your parents about making a plan.

CLOSEMOUTHED

Read about Daniel being rescued from lions in Daniel 6.

HOW WOULD YOU FEEL if you were surrounded by lions? Scared? Nervous? Like a snack? We can assume that Daniel was feeling all those emotions when King Darius threw him into a lions' den for praying to God. But Daniel did not let fear keep him from doing what he knew was right.

When he learned that a law had been signed saying that no one could pray to anyone or anything but the king for thirty days, Daniel went home and prayed to God with his window open "just as he had always done" (Daniel 6:10). The king's advisors watched him do this and told the king. Although the king liked Daniel, he had him thrown to hungry lions as a punishment for breaking the law.

But that night God sent an angel to shut the mouths of the lions. When King Darius came to see what was left of Daniel in the morning, he found Daniel alive and untouched!

Seeing Daniel's courage and God's protection changed King Darius's heart. He ordered that Daniel be lifted out of the lions' den and made a new law that everyone in his kingdom should worship God.

Pray: Ask God to help you trust him in dangerous situations and not be afraid.

> [Daniel said,] "My God sent his angel to shut the lions' mouths so that they would not hurt me, for I have been found innocent in his sight. And I have not wronged you, Your Majesty."
> **DANIEL 6:22**

I DON'T DESERVE THIS BAD DAY!

Read about God teaching Jonah about forgiveness in Jonah 3 and 4.

"MOM, THEY STOLE MY BACKPACK!" Michael said, looking into the backseat of the car. The windows had been broken. Glass and papers were strewn everywhere. "My new history book was in there, and we have to pay for lost books. How can we do that? Dad doesn't even have a job."

Michael felt like God had let him down. His family was at church when someone broke into their car. Why would God let something bad happen when they were following him and worshiping in church? He hoped the thief would be caught and punished.

The prophet Jonah felt even angrier than Michael. God told Jonah to go to Nineveh. Jonah headed the other way, but was quickly hand-delivered in the belly of a great fish. *Gross.* When Jonah finally obeyed God and told the Ninevites that God planned to destroy their city, he thought God would wipe these terrible people off the planet—and he was happy about it. But the Ninevites told God they were sorry and promised to change. So God forgave them. Jonah complained to God, left Nineveh, and sat down to sulk. What a bad day! Jonah felt so hot and angry that he wanted to die. God reminded him that, as God, he could forgive people and be merciful.

God showed Michael mercy too. Michael prayed and forgave the unknown thief. He found a better backpack on sale in a dollar bin at a store. His little brother prayed daily for Michael to get his book back, and a week later a friend called to say he had found Michael's stolen book in his driveway. What a turnaround! That's the beginning of a great day.

Pray: Praise God for his mercy and forgiveness.

> [Jonah said,] "I knew that you are a merciful and compassionate God, slow to get angry and filled with unfailing love. You are eager to turn back from destroying people."
> **JONAH 4:2**

WEIRD FACTS:
ROARING LIONS

- A lion's roar can be heard five miles away in all directions.
- The tassel at the end of a lion's tail is used for communicating. It can signal directions or invite another lion to come close.
- Lions eat only every third or fourth day.
- Talk about a big gulp—a lion can drink for twenty minutes after eating.
- Lions see five times better than people, so don't play hide-and-seek with one.
- The Swahili word for *lion* is *simba* and means "king," "strong," and "aggressive."
- In the Bible, a lion killed a bad prophet but did not eat him (1 Kings 13:23-26).

WACKY LAUGHS

Foolish things thieves have actually done:

- One thief wore the boots he was accused of stealing to his trial.
- A burglar ran from the police by jumping a fence into a prison yard.
- A robber left his wallet with his ID in it, making him easy to find.

BAD-NEWS BEARER

Read about Micah speaking God's warnings to the people of Israel in Micah 6.

HAVE YOU EVER HAD TO stand up to a friend who wasn't acting the right way? It can be hard, because you don't want to ruin a friendship. But a friend's safety and well-being are way more important than safeguarding your relationship. So if you see a friend messing around with inappropriate relationships, smoking, or drinking alcohol, you need to encourage him to make better choices (and probably tell a parent, too). If he's a true friend, he'll know your warning comes because you care. The writer of Proverbs knew this when he wrote, "Wounds from a sincere friend are better than many kisses from an enemy" (Proverbs 27:6).

In the Old Testament, God raised up prophets to encourage his people to live for him. Sometimes the prophets brought reminders of God's laws or foretold future blessings. But many times, the prophets had to bring bad news. The book of Micah is filled with warnings to God's people in Israel and Judah. At this point in history, the people were living for themselves—not God. Merchants were cheating customers. People lied so much that they no longer knew what the truth was (Micah 6:10-12).

God is always loving and ready to forgive. But he's also absolutely just. When his people willfully and knowingly disobeyed his commands and went the other way, God removed his blessing and allowed judgment to come. Micah had to be the bearer of bad news when he said judgment was coming. The people didn't like Micah very much, but they respected him because they knew he always spoke God's truth.

Your friends might not like it at first when you challenge their behavior. But being a good friend means you will try to protect your friends from the harm that comes from wrong choices. Because you truly care about them, you want to help them do what is right.

Pray: Ask God for the courage to point out to a friend when he's going the wrong way.

Wounds from a sincere friend are better than many kisses from an enemy.
PROVERBS 27:6

CITY OF PROMISE

Read about God's promise to restore Jerusalem in Zechariah 8.

HAVE YOU EVER VISITED an Old West ghost town? You look around at falling-down buildings and empty dirt streets. Tumbleweeds blow across the road. Lizards scamper under wooden sidewalks to find shade. You can tell that this was once an exciting place to live, but not anymore. Those glory days of gold, glamour, and parties are long gone. Many old towns eventually disappear, never to be seen again.

During the prophet Zechariah's life, visiting Jerusalem was kind of like visiting a ghost town. You could tell the city had been something special, but it wasn't anymore. The city walls were knocked down. The Temple had been destroyed. With their capital gone, Jewish people were spread all over the Middle East. But God gave his prophet an amazing promise. Instead of Jerusalem disappearing into the sand, the Lord of Heaven's Armies said the city would be restored. Old men would walk and talk in the city square. Children would play in the streets (Zechariah 8:4-5). God knew the few people living in Jerusalem probably wouldn't believe him, because the living conditions were so unsafe and depressing. So he told Zechariah that he'd bring his people from the east and west and once again they'd live safely. "All this may seem impossible to you now," the Lord said. "But is it impossible for me?" (verse 6).

Think about that question: Is it impossible for God? Of course not! Nothing is impossible for the all-powerful Master and Creator of the universe. Next time you face a seemingly impossible situation, remember God's words to Zechariah.

Pray: Thank God that nothing is impossible for him.

> This is what the LORD of Heaven's Armies says: All this may seem impossible to you now, a small remnant of God's people. But is it impossible for me?
> ZECHARIAH 8:6

EXPERIMENT: IMPOSSIBLE FLOAT

Use salt to change the density of water and lift up an egg.

STUFF YOU NEED

- 6 tablespoons salt
- Drinking glass
- 1 cup water
- Egg

TRY IT

1. Dump six tablespoons of salt into the bottom of a glass.
2. Slowly add one cup of water without stirring.
3. Lower an egg into the salt water. It will sink. It may take several hours, but the salt will dissolve in the water and the egg will rise.

WORD PUZZLE

Solve this puzzle to find out what God wanted his people to build once they returned to Jerusalem.

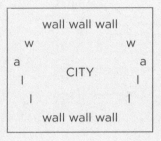

ALL FOR THE WALL

Read about the Israelites bravely rebuilding the wall of Jerusalem in Nehemiah 4.

"YOU CAN'T MAKE SOMETHING out of that heap of rubbish and burned stones!" Sanballat taunted. "You're a bunch of poor, feeble Jews."

"The stone wall will collapse if a fox climbs on it," Tobiah said.

Sanballat and Tobiah were bullies. They teased the Israelites that they could never rebuild the city wall around Jerusalem. The rubble had sat for many years, and no one had fixed any part of it.

Babylonians had destroyed Jerusalem, the city where the Israelites worshiped God. They marched the people to a foreign land and made them serve as slaves. But finally, the king of Babylon had allowed some of God's people to return.

Hooray! The Israelites rebuilt the Temple. *Boo!* The city wall remained a pile of rubble seventy years after the Temple was rebuilt. Cities needed walls as protection from enemies and wild animals. The king let Nehemiah go to Jerusalem and lead the people in rebuilding the wall.

Nehemiah ignored Sanballat's and Tobiah's teasing and threats and encouraged the Israelites to just continue working. Then the bullies moved on to threatening physical harm. That's when the people responded with a great idea. One person worked while another stood and held a weapon. They prayed and stood up for one another. They didn't confront the bullies, but they focused on their own activities and stuck together. The Israelites completed the wall in 52 days.

Even though the people had worked together to build the wall, Nehemiah noticed the richer people taking advantage of the poorer families. Other families bickered with each other. Nehemiah had the priests read the Scriptures and hold a revival. The people agreed to get along. They chose to dedicate the restored wall and their hearts to God. On the dedication day, the people marched on the wall and held a great celebration to thank God for helping them.

Pray: Rejoice that God rewards those who obey him courageously.

Only half my men worked while the other half stood guard with spears, shields, bows, and coats of mail. The leaders stationed themselves behind the people of Judah.
NEHEMIAH 4:16

THE BEST OFFENSE

Read about the armor God offers you in Ephesians 6:10-18.

IF YOU PLAY SPORTS, you might have heard a coach say, "A good defense is the best offense." But what exactly does that mean?

Well, if a team can't score against you, it gives you a better chance at victory. Colin's youth basketball team tried that strategy. They worked hard in practice at moving their feet on defense. They learned about staying between their man and the basket. They drilled on getting good position for rebounds. The result? They won one of their games 36–0.

Now that's playing good defense! Just *one* steal and layup would've won the game for Colin's team if they prevented the other team from scoring.

Just like athletes, knights believed in a good defense. A strong shield was just as important—maybe even more important—than a sharp sword. A shield blocked an enemy's attacks from close range and from a distance. A shield was especially effective in stopping arrows.

God knows about the importance of playing defense as you follow him. He gives you armor to protect yourself and the sword of his Word to fight with. But one of the most important things God provides is the shield of faith (Ephesians 6:16). Your faith in Christ guards you against Satan's attacks of doubt and deception. Hold on tightly to your faith. Use it to shield your mind and body. Your faith isn't just a great defensive tool; you can also use it to go on offense. Shields can be a powerful offensive weapon . . . just ask comic-book hero Captain America.

Pray: Thank God for giving you his protection.

In addition to all of these, hold up the shield of faith to stop the fiery arrows of the devil.
EPHESIANS 6:16

LIFTOFF LIST

Put check marks next to all the ways that you're being a modern-day knight.

___ Being friendly to kids who don't have many friends

___ Telling the truth to my parents

___ Always finishing my homework

___ Respecting girls, including with the TV shows I watch and the things I look at on the Internet

___ Honoring my teachers

___ Going to church

___ Being a leader

___ Making decisions that honor God

AWESOME ACTIVITY: BALLOON SWORD FIGHT

Blow up long balloons and enjoy a balloon battle. Try some of these techniques used in real sword fights and have fun.

- "Drawing the sword" means removing it from the scabbard strapped to your body. Practice starting with the balloon sword at your side and drawing it upward.
- Your body needs to be balanced to fight. Watch where you place each foot.
- It's best to stand perpendicular (at a right angle) to your opponent, so less of your body is exposed.
- *En garde* means to ready your weapon.
- To block is to stop a blow from an opponent.
- To lunge is to thrust the sword forward toward your opponent's chest.

GIVE IT ALL TO GOD

Read about God calling the Israelites to follow him again in Malachi 3:6-18.

SOME PEOPLE THINK the Bible is just a big book of rules. If you read your way through the Old Testament, especially Leviticus, you may be thinking, *They're right!*

The Old Testament does have a lot of rules, because God's people needed a lot of direction. Story after story shows how people chose to follow their own path or turn to false gods. In the book of Malachi, the prophet puts out a challenge. For years the Israelites had wandered from God and cheated each other. They even cheated the Lord by not bringing their tithes to the Temple. God commanded that people give a tithe—or 10 percent—back to him (Leviticus 27:30). But the people didn't like to give up their stuff, so they didn't tithe.

Malachi brought a message from the Lord: "Bring all the tithes into the storehouse so there will be enough food in my Temple. If you do . . . I will pour out a blessing so great you won't have enough room to take it in!" (Malachi 3:10). How's that for a challenge? God blesses us with everything we have, and he asks only that we give a fraction back to him. He's basically saying, "You can't outgive me."

That's definitely true. God proves it in the book after Malachi in the Bible—Matthew. God sends the gift of his Son to take away the sins of the world. Jesus also changed the way his followers looked at Old Testament laws. Jesus came to give us life . . . not a lot of rules. So don't be afraid to give your money, time, or talents back to God. He wants to use what you have for your good and his glory.

Pray: Ask God for the strength to give what you have back to him.

> *"Bring all the tithes into the storehouse so there will be enough food in my Temple. If you do," says the LORD of Heaven's Armies, "I will open the windows of heaven for you. I will pour out a blessing so great you won't have enough room to take it in! Try it! Put me to the test!"*
> **MALACHI 3:10**

TRUTH OR CONSEQUENCE

Read about Zechariah's surprise at the Temple in Luke 1:5-25.

HAVE YOU PLAYED THE "TELEPHONE GAME," where a secret message is whispered by each person around a circle? At the end, the message seldom sounds like the original.

Urban legends start in similar ways. They begin with a grain of truth but are retold and changed until they hardly sound like the original story. People pass them on through e-mail or talking to each other until it's hard to figure out what the truth is. So, no, a hunter in Texas did not shoot Bigfoot, and baby carrots are not deformed carrots soaked in chlorine. Myths and false stories can make it hard for people to know the truth.

Zechariah had heard about angels speaking to men, but it had been hundreds of years since any man had heard from a heavenly being. One day, as Zechariah served in the Temple, an angel appeared and gave him a wonderful message: he and his wife would have a special son who would turn the hearts of people back to God.

"How can I be sure this will happen?" Zechariah said. "I'm an old man now, and my wife is also well along in years" (Luke 1:18).

Oops! Wrong thing to say to one of God's angels. The angel Gabriel told old Zechariah he'd be unable to speak until his son was born. For nearly a year, Zechariah couldn't talk. But once the baby was born and Zechariah wrote, "His name is John" (just as the angel had told him to do), his voice returned and he praised God.

When you don't believe God's Word, there are consequences. You can always trust God and the messages he sends you. And if you aren't sure if what you are hearing is from God, check with what is written in the Bible. If the message you are hearing is different from what is in the Bible, you can know not to trust it.

Pray: Ask God for wisdom to know when he is speaking to you, and for strength to obey his Word.

> [The angel said,] "Since you didn't believe what I said, you will be silent and unable to speak until the child is born. For my words will certainly be fulfilled at the proper time."
> **LUKE 1:20**

PUZZLE IT OUT: HAPPY TO GIVE

Giving away our money isn't always easy. God looks at our hearts when we give. Solve these math problems to figure out what 2 Corinthians 9:7 says.

"_____ _____ _____ ___ _____ _____ _____ _____."

$3 + 4$ $\quad$ 3×2 $\quad$ $17\text{-}12$ $\quad$ 1×1 $\quad$ $28 \div 14$ $\quad$ $1 + 2$ $\quad$ $56 \div 7$ $\quad\quad$ $11\text{-}7$

1 – a
2 – person
3 – who
4 – cheerfully

5 – loves
6 – God
7 – for
8 – gives

WEIRD FACTS:
WHAT'S THAT SOUND?

- If it's too noisy to hear someone talk, then it is too loud for your ears and could cause hearing loss.
- Sound travels through water three times faster than it travels through air.
- Radio waves travel faster than sound, so a broadcast on a radio can be heard 10,000 miles away before it is heard in the back of the room where the broadcaster is speaking.

God spoke to people in the Bible in various ways:

- Through putting a plan in a heart or mind (Nehemiah 2:12; 7:5)
- Through angels (Revelation 1:1)
- In a soft whisper (1 Kings 19:12-13)
- In an audible voice (Acts 10:19-20)
- Through dreams and visions (Acts 10:9-16)

DREAM COME TRUE

Read about an angel appearing to Joseph in Matthew 1:18-21.

HAVE YOU EVER SEEN a dog whine or bark in its sleep? Or maybe you've had a dog whose legs move when it's sleeping. If it looks like your dog is dreaming, that's because it is.

Scientists say the sleeping brain-wave activity of humans and dogs is very similar. Scientists also believe dogs most frequently dream of chasing squirrels or eating a big steak. *Just kidding.* Researchers have no idea what dogs dream.

While dogs have dreams like we do, it's probably safe to say that an angel has never appeared to a napping canine. But that's what happened to Joseph at the beginning of the New Testament. He was engaged to be married to a young woman named Mary—yes, *that* Mary. One night an angel of the Lord appeared to him in a dream and told Joseph to take Mary as his wife because her child was God's Son, who would save his people from their sins. When Joseph woke up, he knew exactly what to do. He'd do what God said. (That's always good advice.)

You may never be visited by an angel in a dream, but you can still learn from Joseph. He obeyed God. He celebrated the birth of Jesus. And he trusted everything the angel said. Jesus did come to save us from our sins! He's a dream come true.

Pray: Thank Jesus for coming to earth to save you.

> *"Joseph, son of David," the angel said, "do not be afraid to take Mary as your wife. For the child within her was conceived by the Holy Spirit. And she will have a son, and you are to name him Jesus, for he will save his people from their sins."*
> **MATTHEW 1:20-21**

WHERE THERE'S A WILL, THERE'S A WAY

Read about a group of friends breaking through a roof to get to Jesus in Mark 2:1-12.

"HEY, DAD, I want to be a mountain climber when I grow up."

"That's a lofty ambition, Dan, but you need to figure out what to do while you climb mountains."

"Huh? I'll just get to the top."

"Son, most people won't even give you a dollar to climb a mountain. So you need to find a way to earn money as you climb."

Dan Doody thought about his dad's comments. He paced up and down a hill and prayed. He stood at the top of the hill and gazed down. Everything looked as pretty as a picture. He thought, *That's it!* He saved money for a camera that he could wear around his head when he climbed. He worked hard at learning how to take great photos. He learned to take a sequence of pictures one at a time as a flower opened or an ant moved a crumb to show the whole process (called time-lapse photography). Dan took such great pictures and learned to climb so well that a magazine hired him to snap pictures on many mountain-climbing trips, including Mount Everest—the highest peak in the world.

Creative thinking helps you find solutions. A few men thought of something new when they wanted Jesus to heal their friend. Jesus was preaching in a house, surrounded by crowds of people. The men couldn't get close to Jesus, so they carried their friend onto the roof, cut a hole, and lowered him down to where Jesus was standing. The men knew that Jesus had the power to heal their friend, so they were going to do whatever it took to get him in front of Jesus. Jesus appreciated the friends' creativity and healed the man, both spiritually and physically.

As you seek God's will for your life, be creative. There are millions of ways to glorify and serve God. Don't be afraid to think outside the box! You may be amazed at how God blesses you when you try something new for him.

Pray: Ask God to give you wisdom and creativity as you follow him.

They couldn't bring him to Jesus because of the crowd, so they dug a hole through the roof above his head. Then they lowered the man on his mat, right down in front of Jesus.
MARK 2:4

AWESOME ACTIVITY: TEAM-BUILDING CHALLENGES

Gather friends, divide into teams, and try a few challenges:

- Give groups egg cartons to build towers that will be tested to see whether they can hold an egg on top without the egg falling and breaking. The tallest tower that passes the test wins.
- Hide jigsaw puzzle pieces with a colored dot on the back of each to match team colors. See which team finds all their pieces and completes their puzzle first.
- Have team members build towers using only balloons and static electricity. See who can build the tower with the most balloons.

PUZZLE IT OUT: FINDING THE TRUTH

It can take people time to understand the truth about Jesus. Find your way through the maze by following the path with the letters "Jesus is the real healer."

```
T I J E L E R  ← END
S E M E A M
  I N H L
  T A A E
  E T H E R
K E R E H T K
  C H A E S
  T L H I
K S U E U S
  I A J S
  S L R
  U E P
  A S
  E D R K
START  J N
```

LET'S GO CLIMB A TREE

Read about Zacchaeus climbing a tree to see Jesus in Luke 19:1-10.

MATEO DRAGGED BIG BRANCHES from the woods and piled them in a large circle. He tied some together to form a hut. Then he cut a slit for a window. Mateo stood back and admired his hideout. It was perfect! But it wasn't for him. As strange as it sounds, Mateo made the hut for his mom. She was a photographer and wanted to snap shots of birds in the yard—but the birds kept flying away. Mateo made the lookout big enough for his mom to kneel inside and shoot photos through the long, narrow slit. With Mom tucked safely inside the wooded hideout, the birds never suspected a thing. She snapped lots of photos as birds swooped down to the birdbath or pecked at seeds and berries scattered on the ground. She took close-ups of birds' wings, beaks, and even eyes from her bird's-eye view.

Trees can come in very handy. Long ago, Zacchaeus used a tree as a lookout. He was a short man stuck in a crowd of people, so he climbed into a tree, thinking no one would see him watching Jesus. *Oops!* Jesus stopped, looked up, and started talking to Zacchaeus. Later, the Lord ate with Zacchaeus, and he became a Christ follower.

Zacchaeus didn't let his height or the crowd keep him from seeing and hearing Jesus, and Jesus noticed and blessed his effort. Is there anything in your life keeping you from being near to Jesus? If so, ask God to help you remove that obstacle. He loves you and wants to be with you.

Pray: Tell God that you want to be near him.

> *When Jesus came by, he looked up at Zacchaeus and called him by name. "Zacchaeus!" he said. "Quick, come down! I must be a guest in your home today." Zacchaeus quickly climbed down and took Jesus to his house in great excitement and joy.*
> **LUKE 19:5-6**

WHY CAN'T WE GET ALONG?

Read what Jesus has to say about your enemies in Matthew 5:43-48.

YOU'VE PROBABLY HEARD THE SAYING "fighting like cats and dogs." Cats and dogs don't normally get along, especially if the cat is a cheetah. Cheetahs are fast and ferocious. They can run faster than 70 miles per hour and have sharp teeth to devour their prey.

But at the Cincinnati Zoo, cheetahs and dogs *do* get along in amazing ways. One of the first examples of this was the friendship between a cheetah named Sahara and an Anatolian shepherd named Alexa. They grew up together as part of the zoo's Cat Ambassador Program. This program helps educate farmers in Africa on how dogs can protect their livestock. Often, farmers in Namibia and South Africa shoot cheetahs—which are endangered—to save their livestock. But a shepherd dog can protect the animals by keeping away these dangerous cats. That way nobody gets hurt.

The Bible tells us numerous times how God protects us. He not only guards us from dangers, but he can help us get along with our enemies. The prophet Isaiah said when a little child (that's Jesus) is in charge, then "the leopard will lie down with the baby goat" (Isaiah 11:6). Normally, a leopard looks at a baby goat as breakfast. But when the Lord rules, he makes peace between enemies. And that's a much better way to live.

Pray: Praise God that he'll come back to rule the world and make peace between enemies. And ask him to help you to be a peacemaker.

> *In that day the wolf and the lamb will live together; the leopard will lie down with the baby goat. The calf and the yearling will be safe with the lion, and a little child will lead them all.*
> ISAIAH 11:6

PUZZLE IT OUT: MISSING WORD

Look at the words below. One letter from each of the first words is missing from the second set of words. Write that letter in the matching space to discover the missing word from the verse.

1. pastry   trays
2. cakes   sack
3. measure   resume
4. cape   ape
5. loaves   ovals

"Do all that you can to live in __ __ __ __ __ with everyone." — Romans 12:18

                    1   2   3   4   5

LIFTOFF LIST

Take steps to live at peace with others. You can disagree, but do it peacefully. Try these ideas to settle problems:

___ Release anger in acceptable ways (run, jump, write about it).
___ Calm down before talking about why you're angry with someone.
___ Pray and think about how Jesus would respond.
___ Calmly tell the person involved what he did that upset you.
___ Listen and think before acting.
___ Meet to discuss possible solutions and list the other person's reasons for what he did.
___ Pray together and forgive the person who hurt you.
___ Choose a solution, then try to set a time to talk about how it is working.

CARE PACKAGES FOR GRANDMA

Read about Jesus' friend Lazarus dying in John 11:1-44.

CHRISTIAN'S GRANDMA HAD LIVER CANCER. She wouldn't live long. Christian's home was too far away to visit her. He had spent many summer vacations with her and had lots of fun, so he wanted to show his love. His family decided to send Grandma little presents to open each day. Christian made a special craft with a note that said, "God will watch over you, Grandma." His family filled a box with pictures they drew, letters, photos, a stuffed animal, and other gifts.

Every few weeks they sent another package. Christian's grandpa said it made Grandma smile each day when she opened another little gift. She lived only a few months, but Christian felt glad that he had sent her good-bye gifts. He would always remember the good times they'd had together.

It's never easy when someone we love dies. When Jesus' friend Lazarus died, Jesus cried with Lazarus's sisters before he brought Lazarus back to life. He saw the pain that Mary and Martha were going through and grieved with them.

We know that believers will live forever in heaven, but it's still sad to lose someone. God cares about you and knows how hard it is when a loved one dies. In those difficult times, you can share your tears, sadness, and anger with Jesus because he understands and cares for you.

Pray: Pray for people who are sick, and ask God to be near to them.

When Jesus saw her weeping and saw the other people wailing with her, a deep anger welled up within him, and he was deeply troubled. . . . Then Jesus wept.
JOHN 11:33, 35

WATER WALKING

Read about Jesus and Peter walking on water in Matthew 14:22-33.

HAVE YOU EVER SKIPPED A STONE across a lake? It's amazing to watch it hop before it sinks. Maybe you can do a double or even triple skip. In 2013, a man in Pennsylvania set a world record by throwing a stone and making it skip 88 times! It traveled as far as a football field before it plopped into the depths.

Another time, some men built a hidden platform to make it look like they could run across the water. They called it liquid mountaineering. They created a video where they took a few running steps on top of the water before sinking in. Of course, they were actually running on the platform—twisting the truth with video tricks.

Jesus didn't need tricks to walk on water. As God, he can control nature. After Jesus fed a crowd of 5,000 with a few loaves and fish, he told his disciples to row across the Sea of Galilee and meet him on the other side. Late at night, as they were still rowing, they saw Jesus walking toward them on the water. Peter couldn't believe it, and yet he wanted to imitate Christ.

"Lord, is it you?" Peter asked. "If it is, tell me to come to you on the water." Jesus invited Peter to come. He stepped out of the boat and walked on water, but only for a few steps. He took his eyes off Jesus and started sinking. Jesus reached out his hand, grabbed Peter, and saved him.

The greatest athletes on earth have never been able to do what Jesus did. The disciples saw the miracle and spoke the truth when they said, "You really are the Son of God!" (Matthew 14:33). Because Jesus is God, you can trust that he can do anything. And when you keep your eyes on him, you'll be able to do amazing things too.

Pray: Thank God for sending his Son to save you and for being all-powerful.

[The disciples] had rowed three or four miles when suddenly they saw Jesus walking on the water toward the boat. They were terrified, but he called out to them, "Don't be afraid. I am here!"
JOHN 6:19-20

AWESOME ACTIVITY:
STARRY CARDS

When you know someone is sick, send a card . . . and a smile.

STUFF YOU NEED

- Paper
- Magazine pictures
- Markers or colored pencils
- Star stickers

TRY IT

1. Fold the paper in half to make a card.
2. Decorate the front with a sky scene. Add star stickers and draw planets.
3. Write, "You make the universe a better place."
4. Inside, write a note and add, "I'm praying for you."

TWISTY TONGUE TWISTERS

Try to say these tongue twisters 10 times without stopping.

- Wonderful, wet, warm washing water.
- Six or seven swift swans swam.
- Sailors swam seven shimmery, shiny seas.
- We'll weather weird weather.
- Sunsets miss sunshine.
- Ships safely sailed in strong storms.
- God's carefully chosen guys cheer.
- Christ came to calm our qualms.
- Toy boat about to topple.

STRENGTHENING OTHERS

Read about Jesus predicting Peter's denial in Luke 22:31-34 and forgiving him in John 21:15-19.

COCK-A-DOODLE-DOO! Roosters are God's natural alarm clocks. They start crowing a few hours before the sun rises. They also crow anytime a noise startles them.

Before Jesus went to the Cross, he used a rooster to wake up Simon Peter. Peter said he'd be willing to die for Jesus, but Jesus knew Peter's faith was weak. The Lord told Peter that he would deny him three times before the rooster crowed.

"No way," Peter said.

But after Jesus was arrested, Peter followed him to the high priest's home. Guards stood around a fire as Peter crept closer. Suddenly a servant girl pointed and said, "This man was one of Jesus' followers!"

"I don't even know him!" Peter shouted back, trying to save his own skin. In just a few hours, Peter denied Jesus twice more. Then he heard, *Cock-a-doodle-doo!*

Jesus used the crowing like an alarm to wake Peter up to his failure and warn him to change. And after his resurrection, Jesus gave Peter another chance to show his love for him.

Jesus did not give up on Peter. He had chosen Peter to have the special job of starting the church, and not even Peter's denial of Jesus was enough for Jesus to change his mind.

Failure reminds us we are not perfect. We need God to help us be strong. If you fail like Peter, confess your sins and tell Jesus you love him. Jesus promises to forgive you and teach you how to follow him better next time. Learning from mistakes and admitting when we fail will help us succeed in the future.

Peter followed Jesus again with a stronger heart for God. He became a leader who preached about Jesus and encouraged many people to believe in him as Savior.

Pray: Ask God for the strength to confess and learn from your mistakes.

> [Jesus said,] "I have pleaded in prayer for you, Simon, that your faith should not fail. So when you have repented and turned to me again, strengthen your brothers."
> **LUKE 22:32**

IT'S NO RIOT

Read about Pilate presiding over Jesus' trial in Matthew 27:11-26.

IT'S EASY for large groups of people to get out of control. Maybe you've seen videos of Black Friday sales on the day after Thanksgiving as people rioted to rush through doors and get a good deal on a TV.

There weren't any TVs when Jesus walked the earth, but his trial almost caused a riot. After the Jewish leaders condemned Jesus to die, he went before the Roman governor, Pontius Pilate. As Pilate sat on the judgment seat, his wife sent him an urgent message: "Leave that innocent man alone. I suffered through a terrible nightmare about him last night" (Matthew 27:19). Pilate wanted to let Jesus go, but the crowds demanded his death.

"What crime has he committed?" Pilate shouted.

The crowd ignored him and yelled even louder, "Crucify him!"

Before the mob of angry people could turn into a riot, Pilate washed his hands to demonstrate that he was "innocent of this man's blood." Then he turned Jesus over to Roman soldiers to be flogged and killed.

Even though Pilate knew that Jesus didn't deserve to be crucified, he gave in to the pressure of the crowd and condemned him to death. He could have used his leadership position to do the right thing, but he was too afraid of a riot and too worried about his own reputation.

It takes courage to stand up for what is right in the face of opposition. Pilate folded under pressure and thought he could wash his hands of responsibility for Jesus' death. But just like Pilate, you are responsible for your actions. When you are faced with a decision between right and wrong, choose to obey God and bravely do what is right.

Pray: Ask God for the courage to do what is right and not give in to peer pressure.

As Pilate was sitting on the judgment seat, his wife sent him this message: "Leave that innocent man alone. I suffered through a terrible nightmare about him last night."
MATTHEW 27:19

QUIZ:
AT THE CROSS

How much do you know about Jesus Christ's death and resurrection? (Answers are found in Matthew 27:11–28:20.)

1. When soldiers mocked and beat Jesus, they put a crown of _____ on his head.
2. Who did soldiers force to carry Jesus' cross when he became too weak?
3. Jesus told his followers that he'd rise from the dead in _____ days.
4. On what day of the week did Jesus rise from the dead?
5. What was the angel sitting on when the two women came to Jesus' empty tomb?

PUZZLE IT OUT: MISSING WORD

Look at the words below. One letter from each of the first words is missing from the second set of words. Write that letter in the matching space to discover the missing word from the verse.

1. lady   day
2. yoke   key
3. drink   kind
4. band   nab

"Believe in the __ __ __ __ Jesus and you will be saved." — Acts 16:31
                     1 2 3 4

RECORD-BREAKING FISH

Read about Jesus blessing the disciples with an amazing catch of fish in John 21:1-14.

GREG BERNAL WAS ABOUT TO CALL IT A DAY and go home.

One last cast, he thought. He threw his fishing line into the Missouri River and waited. That's what fishermen do. They wait. And Greg was a good fisherman. In 1995, he had caught a state-record catfish in Illinois that weighed more than 79 pounds. But on this hot July afternoon in 2010, Greg was about to reel in a giant.

Thirty minutes after his bait hit the water, the reel took off. Greg kept pressure on the line and tried to work the fish to the surface. When the catfish's head finally popped out of the water, Greg knew he had a record breaker. He landed the massive fish and got it weighed. The blue catfish tipped the scales at 130 pounds and was 57 inches long!

The Bible tells a story about a record-breaking catch too. After Jesus died on the Cross and rose from the dead, his disciples went out fishing. They fished all night, but caught nothing. Just as they were about to give up, they saw a man on the beach. "Throw out your net on the right-hand side of the boat," the man yelled. Many of the disciples were trained fishermen—what did this man know? But they tossed over the net and couldn't pull it back in because there were too many fish (John 21:6). Suddenly, John, who is often called "the disciple whom Jesus loved," realized that the man on the beach was the risen Lord Jesus.

Sometimes you might hear a message from God that doesn't make sense, such as "Throw out your net on the right side" or "Be kind to those who treat you badly." But when you obey his commands, you'll always make a great catch.

Pray: Tell God you're never going to give up following his instructions.

[Jesus said,] "Throw out your net on the right-hand side of the boat, and you'll get some!" So they did, and they couldn't haul in the net because there were so many fish in it.
JOHN 21:6

LIFE-CHANGING WIND

Read about the Holy Spirit filling Jesus' followers in Acts 2:1-41.

ONE DAY A $20 BILL BLEW OUT OF KEN'S HAND as he walked to the ice-cream shop. He tried to chase it down, but he couldn't catch it. What a bummer! So much for the big ice-cream cone he had planned to buy. Since it was already gone, Ken prayed his lost money would help someone.

A few years later, Ken deeply needed money. As he walked across a field, he prayed for God to provide for his needs.

Wham! A $20 bill blew right into his face. Ken grabbed it. He looked all around but didn't see anybody. He smiled and thanked God for sending such a blessing.

Wind can do strange things. The Bible tells us God controls the wind. Maybe he even kept that $20 bill blowing around until Ken really needed some cash. That's kind of fun to think about.

Getting $20 in the wind is cool, but the biggest windy blessing came days after Jesus returned to heaven. *Swish!* A sound came from the sky. The disciples turned and saw fire descending toward them. *Yikes!* But the fire didn't burn the house or even singe their hair. It separated into tongues and rested on each of them. They got burned, but not with the flaming fire. Their hearts burned inside with power, joy, and passion. They were filled with the Holy Spirit. *Wow!* God's followers wanted to tell everyone about Jesus, and they did! That day was Pentecost, the birthday of the Christian church.

You may not see the Holy Spirit descend on you like fire. But as God's follower, you have his Spirit working inside you every day helping you to know and follow him.

Pray: Ask God to fill you with the Holy Spirit.

> *Suddenly, there was a sound from heaven like the roaring of a mighty windstorm, and it filled the house where they were sitting. . . . And everyone present was filled with the Holy Spirit.*
> **ACTS 2:2, 4**

SEARCH AND FIND: FRESH FISH

Look for these fish species. Search up, down, across, diagonally, and backward.

H	S	I	F	N	U	S	L
B	G	A	T	S	P	L	J
A	C	A	T	F	I	S	H
S	T	O	U	G	K	E	T
C	R	A	E	A	E	C	R
E	N	U	H	R	A	K	O
R	L	A	C	J	R	I	U
B	A	S	S	T	C	Z	T
T	W	A	L	L	E	Y	E

Bass
Bluegill
Catfish
Gar
Pike
Sunfish
Trout
Walleye

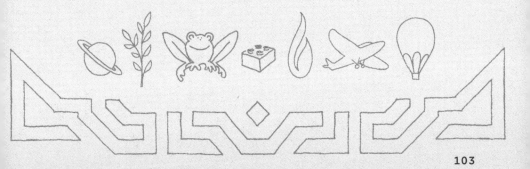

AWESOME ACTIVITY: COLOR TEST

Have you memorized all the colors of the rainbow? A lot of kids do it by using the acronym ROY G. BIV (red, orange, yellow, green, blue, indigo, violet). The next time you see a rainbow, check for all the colors.

And the next time you're near a fire, look at the different colors of the flames. White is usually closest to the source, and it's the hottest. Then come yellow, orange, and finally red. If you ever see blue flame, it's even hotter than white.

Come up with your own sentence where the first letter of each word stands for the colors of flame from hottest to least hot. How about "Boys with young orangutans rock" (blue, white, yellow, orange, red)? Now write your own:

_____

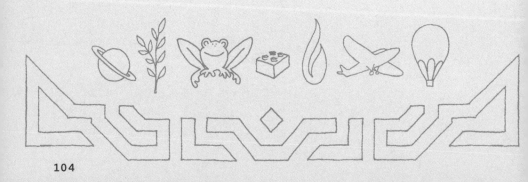

CAUGHT DEAD TO RIGHTS

Read about Ananias lying to Peter in Acts 5:1-11.

LIES CAN'T REALLY HURT YOU, RIGHT? You break a lamp and blame it on the dog. You forget your homework and say your dog ate it. You pass gas and look over at your pooch, like he did it. (Hey, why's your dog always taking the blame?)

Anyway, while a lie may help you escape trouble for a moment, it always catches up with you. Yes, always! Sometimes it takes a while. Other times the truth comes out right away. Take the story of Ananias and Sapphira.

In the early church, God's people in Jerusalem shared everything they had with each other. If somebody made dinner, everybody was invited. If a person needed a donkey, another Christ follower would give him one. If somebody came into a lot of money, he shared it with those in need instead of keeping it all for himself. And that's where we find Ananias and Sapphira in Acts 5. They sold some land. But instead of giving all the money to the community of God's people, they kept some for themselves. That may have been a bit selfish, but it's certainly not the real problem in this story.

The *big* problem is that Ananias went to Peter and said he was giving *all* the money to God. Peter knew the truth, and he caught Ananias in his lie. "The property was yours to sell or not sell, as you wished," Peter said. "And after selling it, the money was also yours to give away. How could you do a thing like this? You weren't lying to us but to God!" (verse 4).

As soon as Ananias heard this, he fell to the floor and died. A little while later, Sapphira came in and also pretended that she and her husband had given away all the money. She died immediately too. *Yikes!*

God takes our words very seriously, and he commands us to be truthful. Next time you are tempted to be dishonest, remember the story of Ananias and Sapphira and bravely tell the truth!

Pray: Ask God to help you always be truthful.

> [Peter said,] *"How could you do a thing like this? You weren't lying to us but to God!"*
> **ACTS 5:4**

STONY CHOICES

Read about Stephen courageously dying for his faith in Acts 7.

WHACK! THUMP! Stones whizzed through the air and hit Stephen. He could make the people stop, if he would stop talking about Jesus. No way! Stephen would never do that. He believed that angels had rolled away the huge stone from in front of the grave and that Jesus had risen from the dead. He believed Jesus was the Son of God. He believed these things so strongly that he was willing to die for his beliefs.

Stephen preached to the people about how God had shown his power throughout history. He pointed out a fact: the people were stubborn. That made them angry. They didn't want to believe the truth about Jesus, even though all the evidence was there—his body was gone; he had appeared to his disciples; he had even done miracles. As Stephen spoke, God opened up the heavens to him. He actually saw Jesus standing at God's right hand (Acts 7:56)! The people didn't want to hear it. They put their hands over their ears and dragged Stephen out of the city.

Instead of begging for mercy, Stephen begged God to forgive the people who were killing him. Can you think of anybody else who did the same thing?

When Jesus was on the Cross, he said, "Father, forgive them, for they don't know what they are doing" (Luke 23:34). Stephen followed Christ so closely that he echoed his Savior's words even as he was being persecuted for his faith.

Have you ever been made fun of or injured because you follow Christ? How did you respond? Follow the example of Jesus and Stephen, and remember to pray for people who don't understand the truth.

Pray: Ask God to help you forgive those who make fun of you or hurt you.

> [Stephen] fell to his knees, shouting, "Lord, don't charge them with this sin!" And with that, he died.
> **ACTS 7:60**

PUZZLE IT OUT:
SWAPPING LETTERS

Swap every third letter with the one before it to decode this message:

Hnoetsy si teh bset hcocie.

_____ .

WEIRD FACTS:
STONES AND ROCKS

Rocks are formed in different ways:

- Sedimentary rocks form from sand and soft earth being pressed together over time.
- Igneous rocks form as hot lava cools after a volcanic eruption.
- Metamorphic rocks form from great heat and pressure under the earth's surface.
- Geodes are dull-looking rocks on the outside. But the insides contain beautiful crystal formations and colors.
- Archaeologists have found stones with eyes or hands carved on them.
- Abraham and Jacob built stone altars to mark where God spoke to them.

CHECK YOUR HEADING

Read about Philip listening to the Holy Spirit and sharing his faith in Acts 8:26-40.

POOF! An angel appeared. Philip had just walked thirty miles north from Jerusalem to Samaria, where he told the people about Jesus' love and power.

The angel said, "Go south to Gaza." *Whoa!* Last time Philip checked, south was the opposite of north.

But when an angel tells you to do something, you do it! Philip spun around and jogged south. *Crunch!* Philip heard wheels spinning up dust from the dirt road. He spotted an Ethiopian man in a chariot. The Holy Spirit told Philip to go to the man. Philip sprinted over and listened as the man read from the book of Isaiah, words Philip knew better than a road map.

Philip asked, "Do you understand what you are reading?"

"How can I, unless someone explains it to me?" the Ethiopian said. "Who was slaughtered like a lamb?"

Philip hopped in the chariot. As they rode, Philip explained that the prophet Isaiah was writing about Jesus. Philip told the Ethiopian that Jesus died so he could be forgiven for his sins. The Ethiopian wanted to become a Christian immediately. He saw some water, jumped out of the chariot, and *splash!* Philip baptized him.

Philip listened to God and followed his directions, even though it meant he had to change his plans. Because Philip was obedient, God blessed him and allowed him to participate in the Ethiopian man's faith journey. Philip had the privilege of helping the man put his faith in Jesus and baptizing him on the side of the road. When you obey God's leading in your life, you never know what awesome experiences he will prepare for you—don't miss out!

Pray: Tell the Holy Spirit that you want to listen and obey him.

An angel of the Lord said to [Philip], "Go south down the desert road that runs from Jerusalem to Gaza."
ACTS 8:26

KNOCK IN THE NIGHT

Read about an angel freeing Peter from prison in Acts 12:1-17.

KNOCK, KNOCK.

"Who's there?"

"Peter."

"Peter who?"

"This is no joke," Peter said. "An angel just broke me out of prison!"

Over the centuries, there have been many innovative prison escapes. During World War II, British pilot Roger Bushell organized an amazing escape from a German prison by digging tunnels. Pascal Payet, a French criminal, escaped two high-security prisons—by hijacking a helicopter both times! In the 1500s, a priest named John Gerard escaped the Tower of London by hacking away at the stones that held his cell closed, sneaking past the guards, and lowering himself down a huge wall on a rope into a boat in a moat. Gerard planned the whole thing with friends by sending them letters with secret messages written in orange juice, which became invisible.

While all of those escapes are impressive, they can't compare to the apostle Peter's miraculous escape from prison. Acts 12:6-16 says the night before Peter was going to be placed on trial by King Herod Agrippa, he was chained to two guards deep inside a prison. Other guards stood outside his cell door and at the prison gates. Suddenly, light filled the dark cell as an angel of the Lord stood before Peter. The angel woke Peter up, made the chains fall from his wrists, and said, "Put on your coat and follow me."

At first Peter thought he was dreaming as he walked past the guards. But once he left the prison and walked through the streets, the angel disappeared, and Peter realized that he was free. God had protected him. He rushed to a home where people were praying for him. He knocked on the door, and everybody celebrated God's provision and miraculous rescue.

Pray: Thank God for watching over and protecting you.

> *"It's really true!"* [Peter] said. *"The Lord has sent his angel and saved me from Herod and from what the Jewish leaders had planned to do to me!"*
> **ACTS 12:11**

PUZZLE IT OUT: MISSING WORD

Look at the words below. One letter from each of the first words is missing from the second set of words. Write that letter in the matching space to discover the missing word from the verse.

1. read   red
2. pecan   cape
3. glob   lob
4. cape   cap
5. flour   four
6. shot   hot

"He will order his __ __ __ __ __ __ to protect you wherever you go."
                          1 2 3 4 5 6

— Psalm 91:11

LIFTOFF LIST

Philip followed God's leading by listening to the angel and obeying the Holy Spirit. Check off different ways that you've seen God guide you.

____ I know the one road to heaven that takes me to the real Leader! (John 14:6).

____ When I'm stuck, I check with God's Word (Psalm 119:105).

____ God moves my sins to another galaxy, far, far away (Psalm 103:12).

____ Today, I did some cool things for someone I loved (1 Corinthians 13:4).

____ God's better than a compass. He can direct my heart (2 Thessalonians 3:5).

____ It's okay to make plans, but I need to let God direct my path (Proverbs 16:9).

DOWN BUT NOT OUT

Read about Paul being stoned in the city of Lystra in Acts 14:8-20.

WHAT GOES AROUND COMES AROUND. Maybe that's what Paul was thinking while the people of Lystra threw stones at his head. Paul had been there when the people of Jerusalem stoned Stephen to death. Now he was the target of people's anger after telling them about the Good News of Jesus Christ.

Stones pulverized Paul's body. The people believed if rocks broke Paul's bones, then he'd stop preaching about Jesus. They left Paul for dead. But nothing got Paul down. With God's power, he stood up and walked back to town.

Paul traveled everywhere he could, telling people about Jesus. He didn't care how mad unbelievers got or how badly they treated him. And they did a lot of mean things to him. Men beat him, whipped him, and threw him in jail. God didn't always protect Paul from danger. He was shipwrecked, left hungry and cold, and dragged out of cities. You can read about some of the other ways Paul suffered for his faith in 2 Corinthians 11:23-33.

Despite all the hardships that Paul endured, he continued to tell people about Jesus. His troubles taught him perseverance and showed people that he trusted God no matter what. He loved God and would do anything for him. When you have problems, remember Paul and trust God to get you through the worst days you can imagine.

Pray: Ask God to help you trust him in tough times—and tell others about Jesus without fear.

> *Some Jews arrived from Antioch and Iconium and won the crowds to their side. They stoned Paul and dragged him out of town, thinking he was dead. But as the believers gathered around him, he got up and went back into the town.*
> ACTS 14:19-20

SNAKEBIT!

Read about Paul being bitten by a poisonous snake in Acts 28:1-10.

CRASH! Strong winds tore apart the boat. *Splash!* Huge waves knocked men overboard. The apostle Paul, his friend Luke (who wrote the book of Acts), sailors, and guards all ended up fighting for their lives in the sea. But just as God had promised them, they all made it safely to the small island of Malta after the shipwreck. The people who lived there built a fire and treated the men kindly. Paul went to put more wood on the fire. Suddenly, a poisonous snake shot out of the wood and bit Paul on the hand. Everybody waited for him to die, but nothing happened. *Whoa!* Now the people on Malta wanted to know more about Paul. They thought he might be a god.

Luke goes on to write that the people took Paul to the island's leader. Paul prayed for the leader's sick father. God healed him. The news spread and more people came to Paul for healing. He prayed, and God healed them all.

Paul didn't worry about his situation, whether he was on a sinking ship or being bitten by a snake. He always trusted God. And he let his actions show his faith.

Pray: Tell God that you want your actions to point people to him.

> As Paul gathered an armful of sticks and was laying them on the fire,
> a poisonous snake, driven out by the heat, bit him on the hand. . . .
> But Paul shook off the snake into the fire and was unharmed.
> **ACTS 28:3, 5**

WEIRD FACTS:
SNAKE STATS

- A herpetologist is someone who studies reptiles.
- The world's longest snake, a reticulated python, can grow nearly 33 feet long.
- The fastest snake in the world is the black mamba. It can slither along at 14.9 miles per hour.
- The carpet viper has killed more people than any other snake in the world. It lives anywhere from West Africa to India.
- The hognose snake and the spitting cobra fool enemies with bad breath. They flip upside down and play dead. Then they stick out their tongues to give off a foul smell.
- Cobras dance to music even though they can't hear. They feel the vibrations.

EXPERIMENT:
SLIMY SNAKE SNACKS

Transform some snack foods into a sweet snake treat.

STUFF YOU NEED

- Oreo cookies
- Plastic resealable bag
- Hammer or rolling pin
- Paper cup for each snack
- Gummy worms, or cut out worms from fruit roll snacks

TRY IT

1. Place Oreos in plastic bag. Seal securely.
2. Use the hammer or the rolling pin to crush the cookies.
3. Place crushed cookies in each cup. Stir in snakes (aka gummy worms). Now you have snakes in a cup of dirt.

Make some to share with friends or family!

WARNING! WARNING!

Read Paul's warning against pride in Romans 12:1-8.

SOME PRODUCTS come with funny warning labels.

A hairdryer warns, "Do not use while sleeping."

A carton of eggs says, "Product may contain eggs."

A cereal bowl comes with a sticker: "Always use this product with adult supervision."

While it's nice to eat as a family, consuming Frosted Flakes probably doesn't require adult supervision. And who dries his hair while he's sleeping? That's just ridiculous.

In the book of Romans, Paul gives a much more helpful warning. He says, "I give each of you this warning: Don't think you are better than you really are" (12:3). Paul knew that pride was a problem. He battled with it himself. In his letter to the church in Philippi, Paul said he had plenty of reasons to boast. He was a pure-blooded citizen of Israel and a Pharisee who followed the law. But those things were worthless compared to the righteousness he found in Jesus (Philippians 3:5-7). Paul could've had a big head, yet he didn't because he understood that everything good in him came from God.

Take Paul's warning to heart. Don't think too highly of yourself. Be honest about what you're good at and where you have weaknesses. Listen to others and celebrate their talents.

And while you're following warnings, don't forget about this actual label on a Superman costume: "This costume does not enable flight or super strength."

Pray: Thank God for his warnings. Ask him to help you stay humble.

> *Because of the privilege and authority God has given me, I give each of you this warning: Don't think you are better than you really are. Be honest in your evaluation of yourselves.*
> **ROMANS 12:3**

HEAVENLY PLACE

Read what it will look like to spend forever with Jesus in Revelation 21.

CLOSE YOUR EYES and picture your perfect paradise. What did you see—a beach? An amusement park? A soccer field? A classroom piled with textbooks? (Just kidding about the last one, but school can be a really cool place.)

When you think about being in this wonderful place, you probably imagine yourself safe, happy, and having fun. You don't picture a hospital room or a funeral home. Those places are usually filled with sickness and sadness.

We don't know exactly what heaven's going to look like. Words can't describe how beautiful, joyful, and fun it will be. But we do know some things about heaven that the apostle John wrote down in the book of Revelation. For one, heaven will be the perfect paradise—even better than what you pictured. We also know that heaven is a place where there's no more death, sorrow, crying, or pain (Revelation 21:4). In your forever home with God, sadness is gone forever and joy rules every day!

Have you ever told God that you believe in him and asked Jesus to forgive your sins? If you would like to be a part of God's glorious Kingdom, you can commit your life to him today. You can't do anything to earn entry. It's a free gift from him. You just need to accept his gift and decide to follow him. You can pray something like this:

Jesus, I know I've disobeyed your rules. Thank you for taking the punishment on the Cross for my mistakes. I believe you died and rose from the dead. I accept your gift of forgiveness and ask you to be the Lord of my life. I want to follow you on earth and look forward to seeing you in heaven. Amen.

If you just prayed this prayer, tell your parents, a pastor, or the person who gave you this book. They'll be happy to hear that you're heaven bound. Then keep reading the Bible and books like this one to learn all you can about your relationship with God.

Pray: Thank God for making such a beautiful place where you'll be able to spend eternity with him.

[God] will wipe every tear from their eyes, and there will be no more death or sorrow or crying or pain. All these things are gone forever.
REVELATION 21:4

EXPERIMENT: POP PRIDE

You're probably pretty awesome. Remember that God is more awesome. This experiment will help you pop pride before you get a big head.

STUFF YOU NEED

- Long strips of paper
- Pencil
- Bible
- Large, round balloon

TRY IT

1. Write Bible verses about pride on pieces of paper. These are some good ones: Proverbs 11:2; Proverbs 16:5; Proverbs 27:2; and Romans 12:16.
2. Roll up the thin strips of paper as tightly as you can and push them into the balloon.
3. Blow up the balloon.
4. Play with the balloon for a while, but then pop it and read the verses.

PUZZLE IT OUT:
UNTWIST THE MESSAGE

The Bible verse below looks puzzling, but the words are just scrambled. Untwist each word to discover how the apostle John describes the place you'll go in the future as one of God's followers.

"The twelve gates were made of pearls—each gate from a single pearl!

Adn   eht   mina   srttee   aws   peur   dlog,

_____ _____ _____ _____ ____ _____ _____ ,

sa   crlea   sa   sglsa.

___ _____ ___ _____ ." — Revelation 21:21

ABOUT THE AUTHORS

Jesse Florea has worked at Focus on the Family for more than twenty-eight years, where he oversees the children's magazines *Clubhouse* (for kids 8–12) and *Clubhouse Jr.* (ages 3–7). He also cohosts the *Official Average Boy Podcast* with Christian comedian Bob Smiley and the biweekly *Official Adventures in Odyssey Podcast*. He has written or cowritten more than forty books, including the *Defend Your Faith* apologetics Bible for kids, *The One Year Sports Devotions for Kids*, *The Case for Christ Young Reader's Edition* with Lee Strobel, and *Devotions for Super Average Kids*. He lives with his wife, Stephanie, in Colorado Springs and enjoys hanging out with his married children and his two grandkids.

Karen Whiting is an international speaker, certified writing and book marketing coach, and author of thirty books. She writes to help families, children, and women thrive. She's written more than 800 articles for more than sixty publications. She's a contributing writer for crosswalk.com and thewriteconversation.blogspot.com. Her books include *The One Year My Princess Devotions*, the 52 Weekly Devotions for Busy Families series, and *Growing a Mother's Heart*. Karen is a mother of five and grandmother of fourteen. She enjoys life on Florida's Space Coast, family, cooking, and travel. Connect with her on social media or her website, karenwhiting.com, and sign up for her newsletter.

GREAT DEVOS
FOR BOYS

GOD'S STORY

FROM EDEN TO ETERNITY

ILLUSTRATED BY DC AND MARVEL ARTISTS

wander
An imprint of
Tyndale House
Publishers

CP1634

The Wormling

A thrilling, action-packed fantasy from the minds of Jerry B. Jenkins and Chris Fabry that pits ultimate evil against ultimate good.

Book I
The Book of the King

Book II
The Sword of the Wormling

Book III
The Changeling

Book IV
The Minions of Time

Book V
The Author's Blood

CP0138